THE POETRY GAMES

UK Poets

Edited by Mark Richardson

First published in Great Britain in 2013 by:
Young Writers
Remus House
Coltsfoot Drive
Peterborough
PE2 9BF
Telephone: 01733 890066
Website: www.youngwriters.co.uk

Book Design by Ashley Janson

SB ISBN 978-1-78203-297-7

Printed and bound in the UK by BookPrintingUK
Website: www.bookprintinguk.com

FOREWORD

Since our inception in 1991, Young Writers has endeavoured to promote poetry and creative writing within schools by running annual nationwide competitions. These competitions are designed to develop and nurture the burgeoning creativity of the next generation, and give them valuable confidence in their own abilities.

For our latest competition The Poetry Games, young writers from across the country were given the challenge to stand up for what they believe in using nothing but the power of the pen. Using poetry as their tool, these aspiring poets were given the opportunity to express their thoughts and feelings on the topics that matter to them through verse.

Whilst skilfully conveying their opinions through poetry, the writers showcased in this collection have simultaneously managed to give poetry a breath of fresh air, brought it to life and made it relevant to them. Using a variety of themes and styles, our featured poets leave a lasting impression of their inner thoughts and feelings, making this anthology a rare insight into the next generation.

Contents

Farleigh School, Andover

Glasgow Gaelic School, Glasgow

Ifield Community College, Crawley

Loreto Grammar School, Altrincham

Mill Chase Community College, Bordon

Miltoncross Secondary School, Portsmouth

Normanhurst School, Chingford

Pencoed Comprehensive School, Pencoed

St George's RC High School, Worsley

Sacred Heart Catholic College, Crosby

The Crypt Grammar School, Gloucester

The Grays School, Grays

The New School at West Heath, Sevenoaks

The Poems

A Teenager's Mind

Nobody really understands
Deep inside a teenager's mind
This world is just so corrupt
That might explain why we tut
But don't blame us for how we are
And lock us behind a metal bar
Yes, I understand we get up to no good
Messing around in our neighbourhood
But would you blame us for how we grow to be?
When there are not many good examples around me
Not all of us are as fortunate
Some are left in major debt
When others live life as they please
We grow uneducated, just trained to tease
The politicians around us
Don't understand the big fuss
That we need to be seen in society
So we can be high not look down with pity
We need to be heard, in order to make change
Get rid of our inner rage
Make us peaceful, make us content
Instead of putting me in a life sentence
We've got contributions to make
For our glorious country's sake
We have talents and skills just like you
Something you should help us to do
As I'm growing older
My passion is getting stronger
To help everyone see
The real inside of me.

Juwairiyah Aftab (12)

Plunge

How is it that a human being has the ability to hurt another?
Have they no compassion or love?
Is their heart a gaping hole of darkness?
Is there not an ounce of regret, or a piece of them that longs to repent?

We live in a world full of hatred and hunger.
Hatred for justice, hunger for justice.
Hatred for life, hunger for life.
Polar opposites of society that stretch us out until one day,
Something snaps and shatters.
Someone cries and something dies.

How will it end?
Will the hunger or the hatred win?
Or will they simply destroy one another,
Taking society and morals with it?
There can be no life,
And there can be no justice,
Unless you are willing to stand up for it.

Stand up and take the plunge,
Before the plunge takes you.

Katie Marrin (15)

Gold To Grey

I wait for a prince who never comes,
In a towering castle above the world,
Keeping me from living

I dream of a home with ivy-covered walls and doors,
A sweet smelling garden and a family

A flowing curtain of gold separates me,
Blocks me without relief

I have to escape
But who can leave without an open door?

Long years of waiting pass,
Until the gold turns to grey
And all is forgotten

All that is left is the tower
And my dreams.

Katie Sawyer (14)
Altrincham Grammar School for Girls, Bowdon

Laughter

Laughter is a hand grenade
Because it explodes when a joke is made.
Laughter is wild and laughter is free
Laughter lives in everyone, even you and me.
I have a poltergeist living under my bed
He is the ghost of an old man not long dead.
Do you want to know what he likes?
Of all the things on Earth, his favourite is laughter!
He can't help it, he laughs all night and day.
He represents the spirit of play.
He juggles objects and burps at full volume!
He writes rude words on the walls of every room!
He wears ridiculous outfits
And he tears my homework to bits!
But despite the facts that he's uncontrollable
His ability to laugh is unimaginable.
Now I do not mean to rave
But I think the one thing he craves:
Is for someone to laugh at his jokes
It's not much but he has hopes
Now come on everyone, sing it with me!
Laughter is wild and laughter is free!
Laughter lives in everyone, even you and me.

Annalise Seixas Sa (15)
Centre Academy, London

Weather

Raindrops
Snowflakes
Sun rays
Hail chunks

This is what affects me
What I wear
What I do
Where I go
Weather, weather
What would I do without the weather?

Raindrops
Snowflakes
Sun rays
Hail chunks

Warm cool, hot cold
Cool warm, cold hot

Happiness when the sun shines
Depression when the rain falls
Sadness when the snow falls
Pain when the hail falls

The sun makes me warm
The rain sends me down
The snow makes the fun come out
The hail makes the slush come out

What would you do without weather?
Sunny days drift and float
Rainy days sog and mops
Snowy days are brisk and fluttery
Hail is havoc and pain

Sun is fun
Rain is vain
Snow flows
Hail wails
I wish for all that weather brings
And much, much more!

Lara Smith (12)
Colston's School, Stapleton

London 2012

From venue to venue,
From person to person,
A bug was sweeping the nation,
Absorbing every heart in the land.
Big or small, young or old, it found everyone.
This extraordinary creature had one sole aim – to inspire a generation.

The nation was a ferocious lion when Mo Farah crossed the line,
As he dropped to the floor time stood on edge,
Too stunned to move the seconds forward.
The city, the country, the world was amazed at his achievement.

But who could forget the fastest man in the world?
How he, as casually as you stroll down the cobbled streets,
In the heat of summer,
Shrugged off pressure within ten exhilarating seconds of action.
The one and only Usain Bolt caught the bug too.

Then we come to Sir Chris Hoy,
Arguably the greatest of all time.
He loves cycling as if it were a child's treasured toy.
Like a true sportsman,
He came from being a sport-craving boy.

Ellie Simmonds' marvellous heats got the Aquatics Centre humming.
Then in the final it was a full on buzzing,
As she sliced through the warm water to take the crown.
She grasped the bug and helped it reach more ecstatic hearts.

Gold after gold after gold after gold came for David Weir.
Like a true werewolf he scared his opponents off with a deafening howl,
The wonderful world-inspiring 'Weirwolf' reigned supreme
On his red hot wheels around the track blessed by superstars.
The bug completed its job and to a high standard.
London 2012 will remain in the minds of everyone who caught a glimpse of it.
They were the glorious Games of 2012.

Oliver Murton (12)
Colston's School, Stapleton

Homelessness

I try to be nice
I'm as quiet as mice;
I do something wrong,
Then I'm long gone.

I pack up my bags and kicked on the street,
Just because I wasn't that sweet.
The streets are scary, there's no security;
I've lost all sense of surety.

I have a big sign
Saying *Please Help me,*
I have a cap with a few coins in
But it only seems to be 3p.

People just walk and give me a tut,
Probably thinking I'm as crazy as a nut.
I walk around town looking muddy and brown,
With a very big frown on my face.

In my clothes there are holes,
And in my shoe soles.
I'm always so cold,
If only I had some gold,
I would buy a nice jumper,
And get my self plumper.

You could make a donation
To the Salvation Army,
Maybe they could help with a home
And I could finally be comfy.

If I could have a new start in life,
I would make some changes
I'd unpack my bags as I have dreamt of for ages
And finally life would be sweet.

Neve Cussen (12)
Colston's School, Stapleton

The Olympics

The Olympics inspired us all,
The amazing athletes, strong and tall,
With their tree trunk legs,
And their sweaty, throbbing heads,
Inspirational, were they all.

Excitement filled the streets,
Who knew who you'd meet?
People arriving from across the globe,
Giving the country anticipation and hope,
And filling up all the seats.

The athletes showed grit and determination,
From all across the nation,
Never more proud to be British,
Welsh, Scottish and English,
This was a time of celebration.

The Paralympians were astonishing,
When they heard the energetic gun ring,
They'd shoot off as fast as they could,
No matter how many limbs they should,
Their bravery was bewildering.

In the stadium the crowd was immense,
With races, jam-packed with suspense,
The roar completely filled the arena,
Everyone watching was a believer,
The competition was truly intense.

The opening ceremony was eccentric,
The stunning stadium was electric,
A time of nothing but happiness,
For everyone to witness,
The Olympics were truly epic.

Rowan Solly (12)
Colston's School, Stapleton

Pursuit

The loudest arena in the park.
I am favourite for gold.
The home crowd are counting on me, Union flags are everywhere,
The crowd expects gold, I must not disappoint.
I must be aggressive all the way to the line,
I imagine myself with the gold medal round my neck.
The boots go on; the Lycra suit stretches tight round my thighs and torso,
Warm up over, time to face the crowd.
Helmet on, feet clipped in – full focus in pursuit of my goal.

The Siberian Pine track is polished to the extreme, so smooth, so slick.
I am focused on the first bend.
The starting gate hooks me up till the beep.
6000 people, 12000 eyes fixed on me, they all want the dream result.
The noise of the crowd wraps around me like a blanket,
Then silence fills my ears.
I rock back and forward for the best possible start.
Beep, beep, beep, beep, beeeeep!
Adrenalin pumps through my body as I explode myself onto the cranks.
Thighs powering my feet like pistons as they rotate faster and faster,
Handlebars locked in my hands, elbows tucked in tight. I'm in full flight.

The roar of the crowd is deafening, they carry me round the track.
It's hurting but I have more to give.
Heart pumping; chest pounding;
Quads propelling; pedals powering me.
The crowd whizzes by in a blur of colours.
I'm in pursuit.
The bell lap . . . the final push. Keep to the red line.
One bend between me and glory, the final burst.
I lunge for the line . . . I look across . . . have I won . . . ? *Have I won?*
Four years of sweat, agony and . . .
It's gold, job done.

George Williams (11)
Colston's School, Stapleton

My Fireman Hero!

A hero; he is chivalrous and courageous,
Night and day, he is always alert and ready to save lives.
The battles he faces are treacherous,
As the wild flames, flicker like deadly knives.
In his suit of armour, he inspires many,
And his strength is bigger than any.

As the phone rings at the station, a beast is born!
A thunder of boots, racing through the hall,
They mount the engine, and sound the horn,
Into the dusky air of night's fall.
A handful of men by torchlight studying maps,
Aware of each second until time does elapse.

Arriving at the battle zone, the scene is a nightmare!
The team leap out, undaunted by the sight.
Inside the lair; the beast looks out, with a menacing glare,
His untamed mane shines like a blinding light,
As he prowls around, he pierces his claws in threat,
And the firemen stare back, through eyes stinging with sweat.

The team, with their weapons, flood into the building;
A cough from the beast, smothering them in his black breath.
Through its scorching path they fight on, unrelenting,
Until their last drop of water has put it close to death,
One final charge and a defiant roar,
The beast is dead, and can harm no more!

Mission accomplished, they return to headquarters,
Exhausted from the battle, it's time to unwind.
The chief thanks them all, and gives the final order;
They leave to go home, putting the battle from their minds.
As I wake in the morning, I hear footsteps on the floor,
I look up, I see no fireman, but my dad standing at the door.

Laura Baxter (12)
Colston's School, Stapleton

Anne Frank

Anne Frank was born long ago
As we probably all know
With an irritating mother
Anne didn't really love her
Also her sister Margot was the same
But her father actually had a brain

Her family were all Jews
Yes I know there are still a few
But at this time we are in World War Two
And everyone was in the blue

Some people came to stay with them
It was a woman and two men
Also a boy
Who then became Anne's toy
Young Peter was his name
Then again they are the same!

Two years went by and they were still in the attic
We are still pretty surprised that the Germans didn't attack it
By now though you can imagine
What has to happen
I admit it pains me
To write down this bit
But facts are right
And early one night . . .

The Germans came and took them away
To a concentration camp and I'm also sorry to say
That Anne along with her mother and Margot
All were a target
To the awful gassy shower
That dominated them with power!

Maisie Cox (11)
Colston's School, Stapleton

Inspire A Generation

Team GB inspired me,
In many different ways.
The way they trained and worked so hard,
Just hit me with amaze.

The Brownlee brothers came along,
And worked together as a team.
They managed to take home a bronze and a gold,
So clearly they had a very good scheme.

And then the best British Olympian,
I'm talking about Sir Chris Hoy.
To take home six gleaming golds,
It must have been such a joy.

Jess Ennis had trained hard for four years,
After missing out in Beijing.
Then she went and secured the gold medal,
I thoroughly relished the whole thing.

Each and every athlete,
Seemed to do their best.
It was as if the Union Jack
Was tattooed upon their chests.

It made me just want to get up and go,
And try out all the sports.
I just wanted to run out the door,
In my trainers, top and shorts!

The athletes did us proud,
They were watched across the nation.
London 2012 did its job,
It inspired a generation.

Sophie Reed (12)
Colston's School, Stapleton

Animal Testing

Animals are dying
For our mistakes
They are no longer living
For our sakes

Why put them in cages?
Why not let them be free?
We are killing them from all ages
From one to twenty-three

Monkeys should be free
Up in the trees
Not trapped in cages
While people get their wages

Animals were not put on Earth to suffer
For our vanity
Not to give their lives to another
To save humanity

From our domestic dogs to rats
Many animals are being tested on
The animals we love and welcome into our home
Are suffering

We have learnt a lot
But there is still more to learn
We have done a lot
But there is still more to do

I hope someday that this will stop
And humans and animals can live in harmony
With each other.

Freya Gordon (11)
Colston's School, Stapleton

The Hunting Blues

Hunting is cruel and drives species to extinction,
For example the endangered polar bear,
You may not think it,
And it may give you a scare,
They are being hunted, for a worthless fur,
Polar bears are playful, and don't mean harm,
But us humans harm against them,
We take their meats, we don't see their charm.

Hunting is sad and very unnecessary,
What about the clouded leopard?
So cute and playful,
People are being their shepherd,
Hunting them for fur as if it were clouds,
The forests they live in are sad to go,
While the leopards inside scatter,
There is a sadness that they can't show.

Hunting is heartbreaking and unjustified!
Another one, the green turtle,
Who loves seaweed,
Their beaches lost make them infertile,
They can't lay eggs on concrete!
So named because of their meat,
Which they are hunted for.
Some people think that it's a treat,

So don't make me plead,
And please take heed,
Don't hunt animals for their pelt,
Their cries for help are heart-felt.

Lucy Xu (13)
Colston's School, Stapleton

If I Could Change The World

If I could change the world,
I'd rid the world of hate,
I'd stamp out crime and violence,
Before it is too late.
Criminals are like rats,
They scuttle everywhere, feeding off others,
Scavenging, without a care.

If I could change the world,
I'd rid the world of hunger,
Starving children with bulging bellies,
Clinging to their weakened mother.
Many are starving and hungry,
While others in good health,
Whether you live or die,
Is dependent on your wealth.

If I could change the world,
I'd stop those who pollute,
And help us to preserve,
Mother Nature's fruits.
To reuse what we have,
Instead of just making new,
To conserve the Earth's resources,
For our children's children too.

I cannot change the world,
Although I want to in my heart,
We can only change the world,
If everybody plays their part.

Benjamin Smart (12)
Colston's School, Stapleton

Going For Gold

The klaxon blows,
The athletes set off,
As fast as you can,
Only one will get gold.

The determination,
The hard work,
All for one possibility,
A gold medal.

Through all the training,
Through all the injuries,
You can only compete,
In the Olympics.

Massive splashes,
As big as a blue whale,
Swimming, swimming,
Can he do it?
Can he win?

All for one thing,
A gold medal,
The Olympics,
The Olympics.

All the excitement,
All the proud nations,
All the proud athletes,
All wanting the ultimate prize,
A gold medal.

Ben Norman (12)
Colston's School, Stapleton

Michael Phelps

Michael Phelps is a cheetah of the seas
A falcon looking to defeat his prey

Determined to be first,
Nothing can come in his way
He is unstoppable,
5, 4, 3, 2, 1 *beep!*
Always in the zone,
His only sight the ripples slowly running away from him.

Everything is in slow motion,
The crowd is a blur
50 metres gone already,
But still more to go!
Suddenly, his hands stop the clock
He finishes – it's all over.
Out of breath, tired
The only thing against him now is the scoreboard.
Has he made it . . . ?

1st – Phelps USA WR!
He made it, *Yes!*
Collecting a World Record!
Drops of sweat and tears run down his cheeks as he celebrates.
He has claimed yet another gold medal at the Beijing 2008 Olympic Games.
Singing: 'The Star Spangled Banner', he stands lightly on the podium

Now it's my turn,
I stand on the diving block,
5, 4, 3, 2, 1. *Beep!*

Nicolas Welmers-Delgado (11)
Colston's School, Stapleton

Suffer No More

Today is the day we get things right
Why suffer? Why not forgive?
Let us be bright!
Let us consider others! Let them live.

The Earth's crying with pain
It's our job to make it stop
People are getting more insane
Why not us?

Mothers are dying of suffering,
The children raised by no one
Why do we have beds? Why not them?
All is suffering, suffering.

I need your help
Nobody cares
It's getting more than I can bear
Please help me now
Sort this despair

I may give up
I've got nowhere to go
I'm empty inside
And nobody knows or even cares

I might as well go away
Doesn't matter if you're here
The suffering has come again
And will remain forever.

Farin Rahbarpour (11)
Colston's School, Stapleton

The Simpsons Poem

There is a family that live in America
That live next door to the weirdest, Flanders
The family is called the Simpsons
Everyone thinks they are funny.

First there is Homer Simpson.
Big and fat.
He likes a good beer,
But could destroy the town any day.

Then his little Marge Simpson,
Madly smart.
Tall like a pine tree,
Though out of many people's league she has many friends.

Then Homer and Marge have a son, Bart.
A devilish little boy,
With incomparable naughtiness
That makes all their neighbours scared to death.

Bart is not the only child, there is Lisa too.
Smart like her tall and thin mother,
The only difference is she is a nerd.
Playing the saxophone, music is her life

Lisa isn't the only daughter, there is her little sister Maggie.
Small and 'unhomerly' cute.
Yet 'homerly' mischievous.
She shot poor Mr Burns,
Apart from sucking her dummy, murder is her business!

Myles Kamwendo (11)
Colston's School, Stapleton

A Nation

The British armed forces,
The heart of what makes England great,
The pennant of this distinguished nation,
The might of a diminutive voice,
Shouting out, courageously.

RAF, The Royal Air Force,
Those reliant, fearless warriors of the air,
The ones who like celebrating those little victories,
Raise your hands in salute,
For those fair, forgiving fighters.

The Navy, are one with the deep blue,
There she blows, across the still and silent waves,
Above or below water, they still come across to be bold,
And whatever you say about these skilful sailors,
They still sail my ship.

The British Army,
Brave and strong like a tiger
But merciful and kind like a shire horse,
Yet with a hidden purpose,
To do us proud.

When the flag of Red, White and Blue,
Flies in the majestic wind,
With all her glory,
I know I'll salute,
Thank you.

Samuel Johnson (12)
Colston's School, Stapleton

The Olympics

When I entered the cauldron of the stadium,
The rest of the crowd . . . the noise was immense,
The dazzling lights, blinding fireworks and jubilant music,
The athletes arrived, dedicated, ready to achieve their goals.
They were ready, they had done all they could to make this dream a reality,
Four years of blood, sweat and tears to achieve this unique goal,
These years had been full of perseverance,
Committed to stand atop the podium.

Then the Games began, many medals to be won,
There were tears of joy all around the stadium,
From athletes and spectators alike.
Those four years of training were spent well,
Finally achieving this magnificent feat,
But when there are winners, there are losers too.
However they do not sit around and feel sorry,
They go out and train again, hoping in four years time,
It will be their turn to win,

Countries get behind their athletes, living the Games with them,
We all feel better, inspired to be like our heroes.
Sitting there, attached to our televisions willing Jess and Mo on.
These are our athletes being the best in the world.
They are on the news every morning, smiling and chatting.
They deserved their medals, so they can enjoy the glory.
I want to be like them, I want to compete.
To commit my life to this would be an amazing feat.

Max Garland (12)
Colston's School, Stapleton

Pesky Foxes?

Fox hunting,
Great idea hey.
All they do is inconvenience us humans,
They can't clean or work,
Nor speak a verse.
They only rip open bin bags,
Steal from our gardens,
And terrorise our pets.
Surely they are the worst species!
Fox hunting,
Great idea hey,
Let's get them all!

Human hunting,
Great idea hey.
All they do is inconvenience everyone else,
They're too busy fighting amongst themselves to work together.
They pollute the air with their cars, their planes and their trains,
The sea with their boats and their oil spills.
They cut down our forests making some of us become extinct,
They never think of anyone else,
Just themselves,
Surely they are the worst species!
Human hunting,
Great idea hey,
Let's get them all!

Ben Fisher (13)
Colston's School, Stapleton

Why Her?

She ran through the woods,
With a cub at her side,
Going as quickly as she could,
She sighted a deer,
And with her preying eye she locked on it,
But then a roar came out of nowhere,
The deer darted away but got trapped tight,
An orange mist came over the horizon,
Then she realised it was a fire.
She ran with her cub faster and faster,
They thought they had got away,
But they didn't know what was round the corner,
Both strolled around looking for food and then *bang!*
The mother darted up the tree, hoping her cub would follow,
But there was no sign, she looked desperately around,
She heard shouting and saw these odd things and her cub,
Her cub was lifeless and alone.
She stared for a second but then *they* spotted her,
She ran and ran with all her heart but *they* caught her,
She was so helpless against *them,*
Why did they want her? What had she done wrong?
Then she saw one of *them* with a hat on,
It was the same colour as her orange and black,
And then she knew,
She knew where she was going.

Antonia Brewer (12)
Colston's School, Stapleton

In The Land Of The Billy Bang Boo

(Inspired by 'On The Ning Nang Nong' by Spike Milligan)

I see the cows going twit-twoo
I see the owls going moo
And the planes going choo-choo
In the land of the Billy Bang Boo

I see pencils rubbing out
While rubbers walk about
And pencil cases just about to shout
In the land of the Billy Bang Boo

I see a dragon playing the Nintendo Wii
While a mouse eats a large pea
And a toilet sits by the sea
In the land of the Billy Bang Boo

I see a tractor wearing a shoe
While a cat goes boo
And a bee goes toodaloo
In the land of the Billy Bang Boo

I see a dog driving a car
While a fish drinks from a bar
And a shark runs far
In the land of the Billy Bang Boo.

Jacob Reeves (11)
Colston's School, Stapleton

Usain Bolt

August the 16th was the date,
Olympics 2008,
He's as fast as a cheetah off the block,
And has eyes like an owl on the clock,
He runs on volts,
His name is Bolt.

Usain is his name,
Running is his game,
He crosses the line,
In 9.69,
But then comes Powell,
Who will never throw in the towel.

When they're training together,
They're friends forever,
Bang! The starter fires the gun,
And they leave behind all the fun,
Because when the race starts
There's only winning in their hearts.

At the end of the day,
They always put on a display,
But when there's work to be done,
He is always number one!

Ethan Preddy (11)
Colston's School, Stapleton

Surf's Up!

If you surf then you are . . .

King of the endless mighty waves but as relaxed as the morning sun.

Owner of an all-powerful board, which you ride on across the ocean
facing the unknown.

You are one of many surfers but so unique in your own special way.

Running joyfully across sandy, pebbly and rocky beaches.
Hurrying to catch as many thrilling waves as you can before the day is out.

Moving fast away from the danger, that lurks beneath, waiting to get you in one
great snap!

Surfing with dolphins, shining as blue as the sea.

Wishing for no better or worse because you know that the waves will never be
what you want.

Finding your way through the shops looking for new gear.
Never stopping or moping because that's not what surfers do,
But you might for a pound or two, to find something that's perfect for you.

Inspiring friends to come and join you on your journey.
Travelling far across the beaches, looking around
But no rock to be found,
Only the castles of the sand.

Oscar Blakeborough (11)
Colston's School, Stapleton

Being Left Out

I hate being last to be picked,
It really annoys me,
In games I'm always last,
I wish someone would do something.

I wish I wasn't last to have a partner,
I wish Miss would just pair us up,
I wish Miss would number us as well,
I really hate being last.

I wish the teacher would number us 1 and 2,
It's always me who's last,
Always in games, class and more stuff,
Who will do something about it?

But why am I always last?
Is it because I smell?
Is it because I'm different?
Well, what is it then?

People shouldn't be left out,
It's unfair on them,
It makes them feel unwanted,
It shouldn't happen to anybody.

Abigail Cathryn Hood (11)
Colston's School, Stapleton

Bullying

Bullying is unfair so let's treat it with a little care!
Calling people fat, that's cruel.
Leave them alone.
Don't laugh at them through the phone.
Just let them go home.
Don't call them nasty names.
Just let them play your games.
'Ha-ha,' why you laughing? It's not fair
People are people, they're living things
So leave them alone and think of someone else rather than just you!

Amy Oram (12)
Colston's School, Stapleton

Words Hurt You Know

That word,
It shot me down,
I felt like a piece of dirt on his shoe.
Words hurt, you know.

How insensitive must you be?
An appalling word like that.
That's not you!
Words hurt, you know.

When I heard that word,
My beating heart stopped.
I couldn't believe it!
Words hurt, you know.

Thanks to you,
I'm in a better place now,
No one like you,
Words hurt, you know.

Now I can start my life again.
No bullying.
No violence.
Words hurt, you know.

Zak Hamid (11)
Colston's School, Stapleton

Dragons

Its mouth as hot as a stove
Its fire will disintegrate anything
Its green eyes look for the chance to strike
Its skin is as hard as a rock
It can change its colour just like a chameleon
Its teeth sharper than sharp
Its tail just like a tree trunk
Its wings as big as a football pitch
Its cave is as big as the night
It's the ruler of the sky.

Henry Williams (11)
Colston's School, Stapleton

The Paralympians

Here's to the people who stayed strong,
When one day something went wrong,
And they couldn't walk or lost a limb,
They didn't give up; they learnt how to swim.

They put on their blades and ran round the track,
And saddled their horses with the very best tack,
Some got in their chairs and raced away,
Leaving their competition behind without delay.

They jumped in their kayaks and rowed down the stream,
Working together as a team,
Some grabbed the basketball, shot for the hoop,
Dunking the ball with a very loud whoop.

These are the Paralympians who,
Never gave up and saw things through,
So when you feel down or a little bit low,
Think of the people, who had so far to go.

Think of the people, who tried their best,
The super humans who proved to the rest,
That they can win gold no matter what,
That they will win more often than not.

Emily Patten (12)
Colston's School, Stapleton

Mean Teens

Life is so mean when you're a teen,
My parents don't get me I feel so alone,
They say I have an attitude I say, 'Life's not fair!'
I concentrate on my image and styling my hair.

School life is hard I get so stressed out
I dodge the bullies and just stick with my crowd
They tempt me with drugs and say, 'Give it a try!'
I spend my life in my bedroom trying not to cry.

My spots are like craters, 'Zit face!' they shout,
My hair is always greasy and I think I have BO
I feel grown up and wanna find true love
But looking like this who will give me a go?

I'm always tired and constantly hungry
I party all night and sleep all day
My world is Facebook and my life is my phone
'You never chat to us,' my mum moans!

These mean teens seem to go on forever
Not a child, not an adult, just a teen!
At times it feels like the end of the world
It is just the beginning.

Ollie Jakeways (12)
Colston's School, Stapleton

Healthy Food

Vegetables are the best,
They make you better than the rest,
Fruits are really nourishing,
Quite beneficial.

Carrots are a tasty snack,
Carrots can be shredded thin and fair,
Carrots are crunchy, chilly and sweet,
Carrots are my favourite snack to eat,

Potatoes are appetizing, plump and brown,
You can eat them with rice or salad,
You can also eat potatoes with meat,
And potatoes are tasty to eat,

Oranges are really succulent,
Oranges are round and sweet,
Oranges burst my mouth with excitement,
Oranges are quite a treat,

Apples are really crunchy and green,
But apples can be round and red,
On big trees they can be seen,
Hung from branches overhead.

Salman Ossenbox (11)
Colston's School, Stapleton

Inspire Poem

She may get tired, but she will never quit
If I have a problem, she helps me solve it
If a bird is trapped, she will set it free
If my clothes need washing, she does them for me

Every day she walks our dog
Be it sunshine, rain or fog
She drives me to school and she's always chatty
She knows we are joking, when we call her fatty

She cleans the house and does the shopping
She's constantly moving, she's never stopping
Dad says that she snores at night
But at least it would give burglars a fright

She does for others and expects no favour
Everyone is her taste, there's no special flavour
She shares other's problems over a cup of tea
If my sun is not out, she brings it for me

She never sees anything in anyone that's bad
She's always smiling, never sad
She makes a dinner that is always yummy
She inspires me the most; she is my mummy.

Molly Glew (11)
Colston's School, Stapleton

Child Starvation

Children's guts are empty,
Nutrients are dead,
Can't think with their noggins,
Brains are all dead.

Parents are leaving,
Leaving out to work,
But for children,
Begging for breakfast.
Children are ignored,
Not even a biscuit,
Not a hot mug of cocoa,
The children walk to school,
No hope to working,
Lessons are starting,
They are fatigued,
Puts their hands up in class,
Saying, 'Miss, I've had no breakfast and my tummy hurts,'
Teachers get their own dosh out,
To buy food for them,
So pretty please parents,
Just give your child a chance to eat.

Leo Berden (11)
Colston's School, Stapleton

The Nature Poem

The nature poem is
A poem about the stars,
That won't involve cars,
Showing what the creatures are worth,
Upon an ever-changing Earth.

The lovely long green grass,
That grows in a mass,
Is like trees to minibeasts,
And little shoots to us at least,
In every dramatic way.

The big and small plants
That grow very prettily,
But can be very prickly,
Pink, yellow and purple,
They bloom in different petals.

The creatures that are living,
That crawl, jump and bite,
Some can see in the night,
Most dressed up in furs,
Hopefully they all purr.

Annie MacDougall-Smith (11)
Colston's School, Stapleton

My Class

Chatter, chatter, goes the class
'Silence' shouts the teacher
So we fall silent
Get out our books
Work, work, work
Read, read, read
Write, write, write
Talk, talk, talk
The bell goes
Lunch, lunch, lunch
The bell goes again
End of glorious lunch
Back to class
Work, work, work
Read, read, read
Write, write, write
Talk, talk, talk
Ding, ding, ding goes the bell
End of school
Yeah, yeah, yeah
Tomorrow is just the same.

Lauren Whelan (11)
Colston's School, Stapleton

Mind Of A Dog

When are you taking me for a walk?
I'm like a boxer that can't be beaten!
When will you feed me?
I'm as fast as a rocket!
Is that steak for me?
I'm cute and cuddly.
I'm incredibly idiotic.
Let me out because I need a wee.
I think I can eat that.
Why aren't I allowed on the sofa?
I'm more interesting than the TV.
Please play with me.
I bet I can catch that bird.
I can hear her but I'm going to ignore her.
If I make myself look cute he won't be angry with me.
Where is she going?
Who's that?
Please don't leave me on my own.
I'm so excited!
Please love me.
I'm a springer spaniel and my name is Monty.

Nathan Campbell (12)
Colston's School, Stapleton

Songs

You make me happy,
When I'm down.
I think you're great,
You need a crown.
I'm always put in the greatest moods,
Just from listening to you.

I've learnt all the words to your greatest hits,
I wouldn't change them
Not one bit.
Many words would describe you,
Clever and amazing are just a few.
You are the best it's got to be said
If they don't agree,
Then they're off their head.

Simon, Jack, Mumford and James
You are so perfect
I even like your names.
This whole poem is completely true
You don't know me
But I love you.

Fenella Ford (14)
Colston's School, Stapleton

Your Family

When you cried your bitter tears,
Who was there to brush away your fears?
And when it feels like no one would understand,
Who was there to hold your hand?
When you were happy and delighted?
Your family was always happy-hearted.
Your family is always there to celebrate
Making sure you always have a mate.
When you smile and cry
They always make a blue sky
When you have difficulties with something
Your family is loving.
Rows, arguments are natural
That's what makes life a miracle.
Mums, dads, brothers and sisters, all of these put together make one big nest
Wishing you all the best.
Love them, treat them like you r life
As that's very, very nice.
Family hold you in their hearts every day
As they love you in every way.

Adriana Hasa (12)
Colston's School, Stapleton

Too Much Conflict, Too Much War!

Too much conflict, too much war!
What is the point?
War is an illness that we pass on.
It must be obliterated, it must be gone
If we do something it could be gone.

Too much conflict, too much war!
Why not put it to a stop?
If we don't there could be nothing left
Too many people have died over the years
War is just like dropping a bomb on millions of people.

James Park (12)
Colston's School, Stapleton

Poverty

We all complain that life is unfair,
But *we* barely know the meaning of the word.
Think of all those poor people in who don't even have clean water,
When *we* complain that ours isn't cold enough.
When we complain that there isn't anything we want for lunch,
At least *we* have the option to have lunch.
And when we say, 'I wish my house was bigger,'
At least *we* don't have to live on the roadside, or in mud huts.
When we complain about having to go to school,
At least *we* have the option to go to school.
Poverty isn't fair, and although we say that we wish it wasn't there,
We still continue our lives, even if we aren't millionaires.
Lavishly and in luxury.
Children have to walk, sometimes even 5km,
Just to get water (most of the time not clean),
World population has gone up, a lot because people need
More money, so they have more children to get them money,
But they don't even have what we take for granted.
I wish that people could all have *our* lifestyle,
But the reality is that they can't..

Amber Willson-Patel (12)
Colston's School, Stapleton

Animal Cruelty

Animal cruelty is unfair
They should be treated with love and care.
Hurt them, kill them as all the hunters do
There are some kind people but only a few.
Let them be free as the should be
Let them have what they need.
So do what you can and all get together and make a plan.
Try to save all the animals
Protest, march, shout,
We must continue without a doubt.
They want freedom,
That's the reason.

Ella Winstone (11)
Colston's School, Stapleton

Defenceless

I wait, alone in the corner,
Helpless, like an abandoned puppy after Christmas.
My eyes bloodshot form tears,
My heart pounding.

Resting my head on the uneven, cold comfort of the cobbled floor,
My palms hover above the tender blue bruises that have invaded my scrawny figure.
My skin throbbing with pain,
My body wounded.

I lie, motionless, afraid.
Afraid of what could . . . might . . . and will happen to my defenceless being.
I wish I had a normal parent,
I wish I was normal!

His threatening words vibrate between each ear,
I remind myself of all the beatings, all the frights.
I feel he is the wrestler,
Making me the vulnerable punch bag.
When will it end?

Katie Sabine (11)
Colston's School, Stapleton

Smoking Is Terrible!

Smoking is dangerous, very dangerous,
This will rot your teeth,
When you first have one,
You will never stop!
As you smoke the cigarette will laugh,
If you have one every day,
Your breath will smell like a dead animal,
Or like a smelly foul, rotten fish, in your toilet dish.
If children are around you,
They will breathe it in,
And they will cough and cough.
If you smoke, you will turn into a smelly bloke!
If you want to smoke? Bad idea!

Ceran Sokhi (11)
Colston's School, Stapleton

Graffiti At Night

From a house wall to a tube train,
It's a clean slate for my artwork,
The stencil is my key,
Spray cans are the tools of my life,

I return at night,
A siren wails,
The leaves rustle,
The wind whirls like a desert storm,
A hoot from an owl,
A stray cat struts,
A fox rummages through bins,
A mouse squeaks,

A cold environment where anything's possible . . .
A beady eye from somewhere,
Sometimes from above,
Or down below,
You've got to keep your wits about you,
The police may be on their way . . .

Elliott Lawrence (11)
Colston's School, Stapleton

School Uniform

Why wear school uniform?
Why bother?
It doesn't express my feelings!
It doesn't say the type of person I am!
Why should we look the same?
It doesn't express what I like to wear!

If we wear uniform the only thing that's different is our self and tie!
Other schools' uniform is more casual!
The head teacher wants everyone to look the same! Why?
Wearing uniform every day is boring!
I don't understand why we should wear the same clothes every day!
I feel like a deckchair!
There are many stripes in my uniform!

Matthew Roberts (11)
Colston's School, Stapleton

My Inspirers Are

My inspirers are
John Terry because he is committed to football
Like a komodo dragon hunting its prey
Mo Farah because he has great determination
Like an ant carrying a leaf
Bradley Wiggins because he is as amazing as Spider Man
Sir Chris Hoy because he is as incredible
As Hulk powering through the city
Andy Murray who takes defeat like a winner
Usain Bolt because he is as quick as lightning
All of the athletes are as determined as birds flying south for the winter

My family because they are as kind as angels
For giving me fantastic opportunities
Neil Armstrong because he is as brave as a lion
Whilst going to the moon
The army because they are as loyal to the country
As the Queen is to her people

These are the people who inspire me, but who are yours?

Ben Horler (11)
Colston's School, Stapleton

Our World

I don't think racism's right!
It doesn't make you good or bright.
What difference does it make if you're black or white?
It's not fair to compare.

In our world we could all stand
In a line hand by hand
If we were kinder to fellow man
And tried to all get along.

Inside he fights thoughts of horror
And nobody shows any sorrow.
But we need to end all this hatred
Now, not tomorrow.

Joshua Barnes (11)
Colston's School, Stapleton

Michael Phelps

When Michael Phelps does a race he always sets a pace
He goes out fast, he never comes last
Everybody cheers as he goes zooming past
He blasts off the blocks and finishes fast
When he goes blast he always goes past
Michael Phelps is the best, he is better than the rest
He is the best and always passes the test

He streamlines off the wall like he is reaching to the sky
He tumbles with speed and power off the wall

He dives with length and height
He glides off the wall as fast as light

Michael Phelps is the greatest Olympian swimmer
He trains day and night, summer and winter
Including Christmas Day
He works his hardest to beat the rest whilst they play.

He has no fear
And wears the latest gear.

Charley Instrall (11)
Colston's School, Stapleton

The Green Lid

Royal Marines not a tale
They fight for us and sometimes sail
They dive out the skies and fly about
Never to be seen throughout!

They fight on the land and on the water
They sometime use a mortar
In 1664 it all started
Since then they have been golden-hearted.

They march in a band
All over the land
I told you it was not a tale
Royal Marines never fail!

Joseph Harman-Bowden (11)
Colston's School, Stapleton

Inspirational

Nick Vujicic is very inspirational,
He has no limbs, people take the mick,
All he has is what he calls a 'chicken drumstick'!

He stands out in the crowd,
Everyone stops and stares,
However he doesn't care!

He is so talented – he can swim, he can fight,
He's not even afraid of heights.
He is also amazing at golf and has a wife,
He doesn't let his disabilities get in the way of life.

Although at times he will face obstacles, he doesn't give up,
He is grateful for his appearance and lives life with a full cup.

He is glad that he is who he is and you should be too
Even with the circumstances he has he will always get through!

You only live once, so live life to the full . . .
Let's follow Nick and all have a ball!

Courtney Foster (11)
Colston's School, Stapleton

The Suffering

People all over the world are suffering,
They cannot say 'Help!'
But look in their eyes, that will say it all,
All they want is your call, it will only cost ten pence more.
People all over the world have it all
But some have nothing at all,
No one to turn to for food,
No one to keep the bugs away,
People all over the world are hungry,
But we sit at home with our bellies full,
We watch the adverts,
But do we do anything?
We want to see them smile once more,
Their country is weeping for your help.

Faye Guest (11)
Colston's School, Stapleton

Nightmare

Tears roll down my cheek, bitter but warm
A rolling wind whips my hair
A dense darkness makes the
World around me cold
A silence only I can hear
Darkness only I can see
Envelopes me in a thick blanket
Of scary secrets
Droplets of fear burn my skin
Fizz of terror wakes me from my nightmare
I sit alone on my bed
My sadness hangs in the air
I wonder if anyone would understand, but would they even care?

Behind my smile I break down and cry
I try to keep my head up but I don't know why
The happiness has now disappeared
Washed away by millions of tears.

Bella Grant (12)
Colston's School, Stapleton

The Girl In The Library

Our eyes meet over the books piled high
She is so, so pretty, oh my!
She has lovely brown hair
And eyes that shine
Alas, she is in Lower Sixth so there is no way she'll be mine
She smiles at me sweetly
My knees go weakly
I pretend I'm working and continue to read
I can't let her know she makes my heart bleed . . .
I know that I blush
The Librarian says, 'Shush!'
All is quiet, you could hear a pin drop
I'm sure she knows she makes my heart stop
Oh. The girl in the library, she is divine
I wish, I wish she could be mine.

Jack Grant (12)
Colston's School, Stapleton

The Olympics

Run, ride, swim, dive
Hit, smash, 4-5
From the barrel of the gun,
Hit the target, gold you've won.

'Run Jess, run!' the whole crowd cheer,
There's silver over there but there's gold over here
Pedalling, pedalling all the time,
Here comes Cavendish, chasing for the line.

Murray takes on Federer,
The tennis hopes murderer
Murray wins but what a rally
Add that to your gold medal tally

Wow what a year 2012 has been
Over 200 countries we have all seen
Some of which we never even knew existed
But somewhere in the record books, 2012 is now listed.

James Tregaskis (11)
Colston's School, Stapleton

The Hunger Games

I'm ready, fear begins to swell through my mind,
The dread of never turning back is lurking.
Now or never, I have to put it all behind,
Evil glances, death threats, silence, my brain,
Jerking.
No one is showing a glimmer of hope.

The horn sounds, the end of life is merging.
We charge to collect our weaponry, mine the dagger.
Once companions, now enemies, fighting for our lives.
Children, murdered at first stop.
I stampede into the forest, my truce already dead.

I am alone.
Pounding, screams, fear . . .
The Hunger Games have begun!

Molly-Jo Baker (12)
Colston's School, Stapleton

My Brother

My brother has left home,
To follow his dream,
To be big in sport,
If you know what I mean?

He's boarding down south,
Having the time of his life,
He trains twice a day,
To be as sharp as a knife.

His dedication is infectious,
As others will tell.
He inspires his teammates,
And hopes they do well.

He's only fifteen
We all miss him so much.
My brother is so kind,
He's the best that you'll find!

Freja Gunningham (12)
Colston's School, Stapleton

Empty

Tanks. Bombs. Guns.
The weapons of war.
Innocent men lying on the floor.
All life has gone.

Crash, bang, boom
The sounds of war,
The screams of fear.

Destroy, ruin, wreck,
Buildings burnt down,
Ash all around.
Nothing any longer stands.

As the sun sets,
Silence fills the air,
Nothing any longer stands,
Ash and dirt settle,
Nothing lives anymore.

Roberta Martin (11)
Colston's School, Stapleton

The Armed Forces

The armed forces fight for Britain
But war is not cute like a kitten
The soldiers, they are brave
Many lives they fight to save.

Often they lose their friends
Others wounded, but wounds mend
Many must feel fear
But know their families hold them dear

But they still have many rewarding times
Despite seeing many crimes
As friends they spend time together
And go on patrol in gloomy weather

They are very skilled
Although many are killed
Even though their job can be tiring
The armed forces are inspiring.

Samuel Bell (11)
Colston's School, Stapleton

Ian Botham, My Inspiration

He's playing international cricket,
He's at the three stumped wicket,
Holding his humongous bat,
And wearing a stripy green, floppy hat

His name is Ian Botham,
He used to play for Durham,
Standing very tall,
Throwing a hard leather conker-like ball

He was England captain,
Made a lot of runs,
He was always gonna win,
Not get thrown in the bin.

I love playing cricket,
He is my inspiration,
I want to be like him,
An international sensation.

Joe Dryell (11)
Colston's School, Stapleton

My Poem

The Earth is getting warmer
The sea is getting high
The land is getting smaller
As we pollute the sky

The pandas are crying
The oceans are drying
People are overeating
The ozone is depleting

Don't kill all the pandas
Or drive Fiat Pandas
Don't chop down trees
Have swarms of bees

Wind turbines and solar power
Not power plants and miners
Drive eco cars or ride a bike
Not beefy cars or motorbikes.

Henry Lidiard (12)
Colston's School, Stapleton

The Rainforest

The rainforest was a magical place but now it's becoming a natural waste,
The sun shimmers through the trees,
It sounds so glorious with the breeze,
The Earth weeps in depression,
To lose so prized a possession.

The smiling sun, the damp green leaves,
Combine together to help us breathe.
The forest is the Earth's lungs itself,
Without it there can be no health.

High up in the canopy nature's jewels are there to see
Under the sky, up in the trees,
A thousand monkeys do as they please,
Insects and butterflies dance and tease,
What would Mother Nature be without all these?
Why are we wrecking this perfection?
Surely it deserves our protection.

Aron Haynes (11)
Colston's School, Stapleton

Animal Cruelty

At the side of the road lay a cat,
A cat who once had a home,
And that cat was all alone.

He had nothing to eat,
He sighed at the thought of meat,
The cat laid in the rain,
Sobbing about his pain.

Under the small shelter left a puppy,
A puppy who once had a home,
And that poor puppy was all alone.

He had nothing to eat,
He sighed at the thought of meat,
The dog laid under the shelter in the rain,
His owners should be ashamed.

Anais Walker (11)
Colston's School, Stapleton

Where Is World Peace?

Why no world peace?
Is it war?
Nobody tied to a leash

Why is there hatred between races?
Is it tribal reasons?
Crazy as it might seem, the colour of people's faces?

Why is there murder?
Is it jealousy?
Too much killing of mothers?

Why is there fighting between religions?
Is it God?
What is the point of terrorist missions?

Does the solution lie between me and you?
We need to stick to the truth
It all starts with teaching the youth.

Joey Martin-Tulloch (11)
Colston's School, Stapleton

Animal Cruelty

Tigers, they're so normal to us, so why do we turn their skins into rugs?

Whales, they're so big, the world's biggest mammal,
so why do we hunt them, turn their bones into medicine
and their skin into soap or perfume?

Deer, they are a natural wild animal, so why do hunters kill them and stuff them,
hang them on the wall.
Fish, fishermen catch fish they don't want,

all they do is throw them in the sea and let them float,
they don't even consider that they are all dead,
So where are they all now?
Look, they're all gone.
The only things left are the deer hanging on the wall,
the tigers on the floor,
the fish floating on the sea and the whales used as soap.

Reef Dickson (11)
Colston's School, Stapleton

A Pitiful Pirate Life

My heart was in a bundle of fear,
The ship wept with damage.
The bullets richocheted off the side of the noble ship
I don't want to do this.
I feel tormented by the death of so many,
Was it my fault?
I don't want to do this.
I've spent so much time terrorising the Somalian seas,
It's my only friend.
I don't want to do this.
The scariest thing is to fail,
Failing hurts deep down, even for us pirates.
My family depends on my success
Pressure!
It is horrible, it happens every day.
I don't want to do this . . .

Blake Boyland (11)
Colston's School, Stapleton

The Land Of What If!

What if dragons were real, I can see them fly.
What if plants could talk, I can hear them singing.
What if statues could move, I can feel their cold grip.
What if cows could cook, I can taste the chocolate delight.
What if jumpers smelt like sweets, I can smell the sweetness.

What if sherbet was everywhere, I can taste the fizzing sensation.
What if the moon was made of cheese, I can smell that pong!
What if lamp posts could eat, I can see them eating everything in their path.
What if the wind spoke, I can hear it speak a language of gibberish.
What if drums could play themselves, I can feel the vibrations.

But in the land of What If nothing is quite as it seems,
Anything is possible in the land of What If,
So next time you go for a wander,
You stop, you look and you ponder,
Always think of the land What If!

Kieran Maloney (11)
Colston's School, Stapleton

You Shouldn't Judge People Simply On Appearance

She's meant to clean
What's that supposed to mean?
He's meant to work
What's the perk?

To support his wife and kids
That's what he did
So she can go shopping,
When all she wants is a chance

And that's what he's stopping.

So what if he wants to moan,
He can stay at home.
He can do anything he wants,
Not just this once.

Someone else can step in,
He doesn't only ever drink gin.
What if he doesn't want to go to war?
He can be the one that goes to the store!

Bam! He's killed,
Why? Because he's black.
Whack! She doesn't get a vote,
Why? Because she's a woman.
Thud! He can't cry,
Why? Because he's a man.

A woman doesn't have to be weak
She's allowed to speak!
A man doesn't have to be strong
It doesn't mean he's wrong!
The colour of your skin shouldn't make a difference,
You shouldn't judge people simply on appearance.

Lily Rogers (14)
d'Overbroeck's College: Leckford Place, Oxford

The Youth Of Today

Some people say
The youth of today
Are shallow consumerists
And they're certainly not humorists.
The youth of today
Are a sea of grey
Ruining our society
Creating anxiety.

Some people say
The youth of today
Are a controversial matter
And then have a long natter . . .

Where would we learn from? What would we do?
You may think we don't care about you
But we really do, and yes,
The youth of today, have crime
And all sorts of slime
Written across their name
But in the end
We're all the same

We are the youth of today
That's all we want to say
Don't look down your noses
We're a group that society overexposes
One day we'll be old
Old, but gold
We're not planning on complaining
And constraining
The youth of today
The 'sea of grey'.

Ellie Arden (12)
d'Overbroeck's College: Leckford Place, Oxford

Why Should Humans Come First?

Imagine living, living just so you can die
Being trapped in tiny, tiny cages
Just . . . so you can die
Just so you can be eaten by an animal bigger than yourself
That is one of the things that has to be stopped.

Imagine you were a mouse, crawling through endless houses
Searching for food.
Then you see something, you crawl closer
You take a little nibble
And *snap!*
Your life is over.

Imagine you live in a huge, beautiful forest
In the trees where you can look up to the sky
Until your home is chopped down.
Everything is lost
You have nowhere to go.

Imagine you were a bird
A beautiful exotic bird.
You deserve to be free
Flying around and enjoying yourself
But no, you are trapped in a cage
All on your own.

Imagine
Imagine all those things
It's unfair
Is it not?
But we don't care . . .

Mara Talbot (11)
d'Overbroeck's College: Leckford Place, Oxford

Equal Rights

He walks with his head down, his face he constantly covers,
He feels totally ashamed, does not communicate with others,
For he knows for a fact, that when he lifts his eyes,
He'll feel nothing but hate, from the other normal guys.
Their disgraced looks, only erode his good heart away,
As he walks past, they ask him; 'Does your life deserve another day?'
Horrendously hurt heart, severely severed soul,
He goes home to his mummy, he is only six years old.
He asks her why he's different, why his skin is patched with white,
She replies, 'My baby, you have albinism' as he begins to cry.
She holds him to her chest, says, 'I love you no matter what.'
He is now in hysterics, his skin feels burning hot.
The next day he returns, to the unwelcoming place called school,
They're being especially horrible, they're being unreasonably cruel.
He continues to show his hurt, as he already knows the drill,
The more he acts ignorant, the more they wish to kill.
This time he is wrong, his blatant pain just makes them mad,
Bang! Smack! Bang! They beat him 'til his eyes are black.
'At least you have some colour now,' they walk away laughing,
The boy can take no more, he runs away trembling.
A rope, a tree and a stool, are all that he requires,
His decision is final, this life just makes him tired.
His mum returns home, finds her baby boy hanging,
She melts to the ground, her heart and soul feels pounding.
Do not discriminate, because someone is different,
Imagine having to live, knowing that you're the reason.
The reason they took their life, the reason that they're dead,
The reason they can't properly function, simply because they're scared.
Whether a person is black, white or pink or blue,
We are all equal, that person is just like you.

Cole Thornicroft (15)
d'Overbroeck's College: Leckford Place, Oxford

Our Careless Sleep

Humans are the brightest living things on Earth,
We have a gift, straight form the Lord, that makes us unique,
In the past century we have realised this,
So we have used it, solely, for our advantage . . .

'We are the rulers of the world,' we decided,
Took the life and joy of all other living things,
Like a bloodthirsty tiger stealing a baby calf from its herd,
Only because it's simple, only because it's for us.

We exterminated all the Earth's breath-taking beings,
Ka blam! 'No useless animals are needed here!'
Ka thunk! 'No more plants, let us make buildings!'
Ka pow! 'Let us pollute, nothing will be left after we all die . . . !'

You should all realise that without animals we couldn't survive!
Without plants we couldn't even breathe!
Even though all this is completely and most infinitely true!
Us, the leading species, don't care, because we're still asleep!

So wake up now, please, open your eyes!
End the everlasting floods clashing down my face!
Help the death-grazing species that can still be saved!
Stop this endless nightmare that is infecting the world like disease!

Please start acting like living things!
Anything to help other beings!
If everyone would even do the tiniest of a thing it would do!
But humans don't care . . . they just tell themselves that they're the leading species.

Pedro Naranjo (13)
d'Overbroeck's College: Leckford Place, Oxford

The Media And Us

People think we teenagers are hooded gangsters,
With graffiti cans and
Hooded jumpers
You think we drink, smoke and do drugs
But, actually we're not like that!

You think we ruin the city with spray-paint
You think we walk around in hoods
With our pants down low, and
You also think we commit crimes
But, actually we're not like that!

You think we're aggressive
You think we're not impressive
You think we're wild like bulls
But, actually we're not like that!

The media portrays us like
Gangsters with,
Hoods,
Low-riding jeans,
And abusive looks
But, actually we're not like that!

We are good people,
We are learners,
You once were like us
The media is wrong,
Because we are like that!

Tahmid Hoque (13)
d'Overbroeck's College: Leckford Place, Oxford

Forests, Fields And Rivers

Standing in an emerald forest,
I should hear: birds calling sweetly,
Small animals scampering through the fallen leaves,
Gentle alert calls from prey.

But no! I can hear:
Thud! Trees falling, the last birds sing,
Animals escaping and calling for help.

Lying in the golden corn of a field,
I should hear: harvest mice working on homes,
Farm animals' traditional noises,
And the corn swaying in the wind.

But no! I can hear: the sound of houses being built,
Roads being paved over the field,
And harvest mice fleeing.

Looking in an ice-cold river,
I should see: the shimmer of an apricot fish,
The colour of a water lily
And the reflection of the river glistening on the trees.

But, no! I can hear: the sound of water being polluted,
Fish struggling to find fresh water,
And the sound of birds taking off.

Animals' homes are being demolished,
Where they live is no longer,
Stop and think before you act!

Amelia Weeks (11)
d'Overbroeck's College: Leckford Place, Oxford

Before It's Too Late

Animals – soon there'll be none left
Because of us

We kill and hunt these precious creatures
For our own needs.
We want polar bear skins and crocodile purses
To satisfy our greed.

Pandas, tigers, lemurs, turtles will all soon be gone
The black hide of rhinos and whales of blue
The only animals we'll soon see
Will belong in a zoo.

We can wear fake fur coats and muffs
Wear anoraks instead
Innocent animals don't deserve to die
While crocodile tears we shed

Animals we love are falling like raindrops
Because we want their clothes
We have our own, do we really need theirs?
Stop raining down those killing blows.

They suffer, but we still kill them, for medicine and fashion
They cannot make a fuss
We are making them endangered
Only thinking about us.

Animals – are there any left?
Because of us.

Cassie Senn (13)
d'Overbroeck's College: Leckford Place, Oxford

24/7

You have nothing to fear, nothing entirely,
That is of course if you are a benefit to society,
But if you're not, if you're a corrosive material,
Then fear me and others with my mentality.

Nothing about you is real; it's just so damn fake,
It's getting to the point when your parents don't care,
A generation of hate, years of breeding animals with no morals,
Don't try to pull back now, it's all too late.

So pretend you have relationship issues, drink yourself silly.
You're only thirteen, you're so pathetic, it's funny,
Look at you and your lads, getting smashed, smoking hash, what a great party,
Yeah, think it's funny to degrade women, in any way possible,
Grow up! Get past your mental obstacle.

You use sites like Facebook, Twitter as well,
You anger me, you're going to Hell,
And so is the mindless nation, that walks reading your posts.

Then you singers complain about how you're harassed,
Can't you see? They're acting possessed,
Stop fuelling them with everything you do,
Don't tell me that's not why, I know it's true.

So here I beg you not to ruin the world even more, you youths of today,
I beg you to stop beating people up, or making fun of the gay,
Because you sound stupid and are trying to show off,
So I'll tell you for the last time, enough is enough.

Jake Rose (13)
d'Overbroeck's College: Leckford Place, Oxford

Olympics And Paralympics

Before they arrive and show their pride, striving for the ultimate prize.
They must go through the tears with not many beers.
Hurting and hating, shouting and swearing, all the time never ceasing.
When their coach says 'Eat fruit not fries,' they think,
Why oh why do I have to comply?
Trying to pursue what they have always been dreaming.
When they finally arrive they are greeted by only a few but welcomed by many.
They are the best in the kingdom, sent by their state to compete in the contenders ring.
They halt and linger on the sidelines, they will inflate while having a debate with an official because of the wait.
The pause before the moment that has been so prepared for, time after time they have practised.
When it comes they must run, they must jump and they must punch like never before them.
We will sit on the edge of our seats waiting, watching and anticipating.
Then we will shout, scream and cheer for one of our great dears.
As they cross the line everyone along the coastline will shine and say,
'Get them some wine.'
When they return to their daily lives some will uphold something very gold.
After the fun and all the excitement we'll move on with our lives and forget all about them.
But they will keep on training and perfecting, some will be ageing and others will be bailing.
No matter what though they will be back in Rio.

Jack Constant (15)
d'Overbroeck's College: Leckford Place, Oxford

Homeless And Rich

You live in mansions,
They live in the streets
They're treated badly, you're treated greatly
They go to Poundland, that's if they're lucky
You go to Harrods, that's normal for you, would you agree?

The people we are talking about are the rich and the poor
The poor are homeless and the rich are not
The footballers are the rich, we look up to them but we are fooled by what they are really like on the football pitch.

The homeless are not having good lives, some might be good at working, some not,
But because they are not having great lives they will want to change that by working to get out of the streets and turn the page.

The homeless do have talent.
They're thankful for what they get, when they get something they will give you a 'Thank you.'
The homeless don't mind what job they get
Being a bin man, that's fine for them.
For the rich though, that's horrible.
The homeless are grateful, the rich have go – it has to be done their way.
No money for the poor or charity, flashy car and house. *Ring-a-ding-ding* the servant arrives.
Cling-clang-cling the coin drop. They will make the most of that I'm sure.

Gregory Weeks (11)
d'Overbroeck's College: Leckford Place, Oxford

Soldiers

I ask you to stand and remember
Both the injured and those lost in the war
I ask you to keep count with me
Of all the wars and lives they cost
I ask you gratefully to be silent with me
Quietly grieve for those lost
As I expect you to show respect
And acknowledge the life that still remains in our soul
I ask that you wish them well with me
All those still risking their all
And I ask that you remember with me
The names of those that fall
I expect that you are proud like me
Of this great nation of ours too
So enjoying all its freedoms like me
Support those who constantly fight for you
I hope that you are hopeful like me
That we'll bring an end to all this fighting
So you'll have to stand no more with me
And mourning families no different from yours
Until then be thankful you can stand with me
Thinking of those who now cannot
For standing here today with me
At least we show they will never be forgotten.

Anandkumar Badiani (15)
d'Overbroeck's College: Leckford Place, Oxford

Melting Globe

Thin sheets of ice cover the oceans
Everything but pollution begins to seize
Plants start to evolve yet waters flood homes,
Still nobody does their part.

The warming sun surrounds us
Whilst the cracked atmosphere consumes us
The government thrive to save the kelp
But fail, despite the excuse that every little helps.

Mia Lewin (16)
d'Overbroeck's College: Leckford Place, Oxford

School

Locked in jail for not one offence
The sentence is years – 11 at least.
The work is so useless, it doesn't make sense
Tick tock the biological clock.

The school is so blank
We learn and we learn,
Yet at the end it's just to be memorised
Tick tock the biological clock.

It's not just school, you'd be surprised
It's politics too. I bet you never knew,
Not just exams they want us to pursue
It's sport as well they want us to do
Tick tock the biological clock.

The carnivorous exams we pass well or not,
Facts, figures, just theory
Is what we learn, worthless, and a waste?
Tick tock the biological clock.

In the end is it worth it not?
Can we save ourselves from the dark, scary world?
First aid, survival and handyman skills
Tick tock the biological clock.

Peter Ulijaszek-Scott (15)
d'Overbroeck's College: Leckford Place, Oxford

Perfection

He stands alone, blasted landscape framing
An epic of abysmal perfection
In his twisted vision, eyes decaying
Through such application of excision
By such flawed genius akin to his.

Alone he wanders, through deserts of glass,
Through cities murdered, down silent roads
Radiation-bathed boulevards, friendless
In towns painted red, unremembered mode
Known but to authors of such brilliance.

Joyous he stands in the wake of beauty,
Only seen to he, in fading echoes
Of this grand opera of fulfilled duty.
Watching as the majestic shockwaves flows
Through still yet smouldering nuclear ash

The forgotten soldier stands here in death,
Yet he stands anywhere in this world,
Time meaningless, life devoid of breath
Stained with images, rockets as they twirled
Through blue skies and to choruses of screams.

Perfection.

Ethan Clay (15)
d'Overbroeck's College: Leckford Place, Oxford

Student Spectrum

In room 21 sits pupil number three,
He has no school equipment, or none to be seen.
Wasted are the words of wisdom from the teacher
Upon the child's ears, like an atheist listening to a Christian preacher.
Grey walls of the classroom mock the boy,
Coats on pegs shrug their shoulders, they too feel no joy.
For the bell to ring, at the end of the day,
Is what the boy waits for, then he can lead his own mind astray.
He'll burst through the door and outside air inhale,
Trying to forget about his maths exam, knowing deep down that he's failed.

Yet, in room 17 sits pupil number nine,
Frantically writing and planning his time.
For he loves to learn; what better to do?
English or maths, never asking for a clue.
The classroom is friendly, welcoming him every day.
He celebrates his exam results with a high-pitched 'Hooray!'
Although despised by his classmates for being so clever,
He is never bothered; he succeeds in his every endeavour.
At the end of the day, the school bell will screech.
Now he's so sad, for no longer can he reach
His essay or poem, to perfect it with an extra word.
Why he is not allowed to is, to this pupil, absurd.

Oliver Green (16)
d'Overbroeck's College: Leckford Place, Oxford

Bird Apocalypse

The new year was upon us
The celebrations had begun
But in the sky blackbirds did fly
In a frenzy they had spun

As fireworks danced, flew throughout the night
A shadowy storm aroused
With all the light the birds had a fright
As thousands fell out of the sky

The morning after New Years Eve
The news began to spread
5000 birds found, all of them dead
Had the end begun?

Theories flew around the place
From great plagues to poison
When the truth came out the people did shout
For the truth was somewhat shocking

When the birds settled down for the night
The fireworks banged and popped
With no night vision the birds had a collision
With anything in their way.

Thomas Ford (11)
d'Overbroeck's College: Leckford Place, Oxford

Chopping Down Trees

The trees have been chopped down, the forest is bare
It used to be the habitat of the rare tree frog
The people who chopped down the trees don't really care
They have turned it into a muddy bog.

If you hear the word *timber!* Then that's a warning
The baby orang-utan is nowhere to be seen
Trees are being chopped down why? Global warming
The mother orang-utan looks everywhere
There's one place she hasn't been.
She disappears into the jungle, searching in vain.

Ellie Hull (11)
d'Overbroeck's College: Leckford Place, Oxford

Tick, Tock

Tick tock goes the clock. Time's running out,
Faster than a heartbeat or a blink of the eye.
There's no time to cry, or to scream or to shout,
Nor to rant and to rave, only to run.

Tick tock another light has gone out,
Snuffed by a wind of uncertain decisions.
Carried away by a sea of despair,
To be buried six feet underground.

Tick tock goes the clock. The bomb's
Counting down the seconds until it goes *boom!*
But we are running forwards, not away.
Towards worlds shattered and blistered.

Tick tock goes the clock. Time's running out,
But we started the path we are on,
And cannot stop our collision course
Towards what we fear most.

Tick tock goes the clock
Tick tock time has run out.
Tick tock tick tock.

Edith Scott (15)
d'Overbroeck's College: Leckford Place, Oxford

Human Rights

I am the light the world has been waiting for, the one who will say,
'This is enough'
I am the rights, the human rights and this is what I proclaim
That any human, man, woman or child is special
They all are able to say what they say, think what they think and feel what they feel
To have a family, love who they want and make a family if they want
This is my property, my space, my privacy and you can't intrude
I should not be discriminated by age, colour, race or hair
I may speak what I want and say what I feel or object to something
This is our new life with free health service protection and a right to life.

Beatrice King (12)
d'Overbroeck's College: Leckford Place, Oxford

Global Warming

Splash! Crumble . . . crash!
Another glacier has fallen.
The water rises yet again.

Whimper, whimper, squeal!
The sounds of a small polar bear,
Like a baby whining for milk.

Stomp, pat, pat, pat,
This year will be even harder.
Food is scarce.

Crackle . . . slosh . . .
The ice melts slowly, but not slow enough
The snow changes from a blanket to a pool.

Whoosh! Swish!
The wind comes again, but warmer.
Temperatures are rising quickly.

Help! Help! Splash
Time is running out, it's all our fault
We must change our actions . . .

Laurel Benjamin (13)
d'Overbroeck's College: Leckford Place, Oxford

Under The Bridge

I was walking along the street.
Wearing my torn-up clothes.
As I was walking along I went to a bridge.
As I lay down I fell asleep into Heaven.
I just finished college and on the road to success.
I was looking for jobs and there was a lot on offer for me.
There was window cleaning and working in a café.
I would never ask for more.
I chose to work in a café.
I got a lot of money.
There was me working and taking people's orders.
I loved it.
The food was great to keep me going.
Three cheese sandwiches a day.
And my dream home.
A tiny apartment in London.
I'm living in paradise.
And as I woke up I realised
That it was just another dream
Outside, in the dark, no security, under the bridge.

Jac Michael (11)
d'Overbroeck's College: Leckford Place, Oxford

The X Factor

Scared, nervous, excited.
A brightly lit stage.
A sea of expectant faces,
I enter . . .
Silence
I begin . . .
The chance of wealth and fame,
Rounds of auditions completed.
My big chance to impress,
Only one can win,
Only one can be rich and famous,
The rest have their dreams shattered, crushed and broken
(by one person – Simon Cowell).
From millions now down to three,
The final stage.
I can do it.
It will be me.
A thunderous cheer.
It is me!

Benji Godley (13)
d'Overbroeck's College: Leckford Place, Oxford

Charity

Charity is like a tree.
It takes in poor and grows,
It grows until it gets too big
There are no more poor to feed the tree
And the tree starts to die.
Then politics comes in and ruins it all
And people lose their jobs
The people who lost their jobs come back
Then the tree is needed again
To take the poor in and get their jobs once more.
Then the cycle goes again until the poor can keep their jobs
Then the charity dies forever because the poor people are no longer poor
Then the tree dies and turns into foundations for other trees to grow.

Jack Turner (11)
d'Overbroeck's College: Leckford Place, Oxford

The World Is Your Oyster . . .

A bird, bristling bright with plumage,
A lizard of damp green,
A dark silent shape surveys his prey
Patient, and poised, and unseen.

A streak of silver, gold or blue
Darts swiftly above the seabed;
A subtle, springy deer, nimble and hesitant to tread,
While high against the midday sky the sinister lofty eagles fly.

Trees whisper peacefully in the caress of the sun.

Crash! Down came those trees;
Fresh scars on the ground
A battle has started,
No peace to be found.

The winner is Man, but what is the gain?
A world that is empty, a desert of pain
And now with all plants and all animals dead
The fault is all ours; it's all on our head.

Jamie Jackson Jessel (13)
d'Overbroeck's College: Leckford Place, Oxford

Global Warming

Pollution is a dreadful thing
Destroying plants oh ever so green
So far we have no solution
From this toxic vile pollution
From this animals die in pain
These facts are quite insane
We are in a real mess
And should be telling folk
But instead we think it's a joke.
We should be taking this as a warning
Scientist have to get up every morning
To work out this terrible problem
That is global warming.

Jack Chipper (13)
d'Overbroeck's College: Leckford Place, Oxford

Homework

Homework is bad
Teachers say it's good for you
But I think it should be banned,
Wrecks weekends (quite a few)
Ruins holidays (makes me mad).

So now I'll lay bare for al to see
Why homework annoys me.
Always mine (plain to see)
Always nagging (how annoying can it be?)

Oh teachers,
Why do you have it in for me?

It's just a test on what you know
It should be left for exams to show.

You know what, I think teachers hate it too
All the marking and bad excuses
How is it possible for one thing
To wreck absolutely everything?

Will Calvert (13)
d'Overbroeck's College: Leckford Place, Oxford

Crash And Burn

And so it begins . . .
Rolling out the machines of death
To hack, chop and burn the tropical fern
To achieve and earn what they 'clearly' deserve.

To bring the wood to be preserved as tables and chairs
Like bodies in a morgue
Kept in coffin-like ownership of the naïve and mortal owner
These cut and composed corpses crafted to serve
The subconscious mercenary armies of logging workers
Destroying the plant under our noses.

So when you next buy wood, think about where it once stood.
All its majesty and valour, hacked away, instantly devoured.

Finlay Currie (15)
d'Overbroeck's College: Leckford Place, Oxford

Global Warming

Many people have complained,
About the world we have today.
Pollution here, melting there,
This planet is about to tear.

As people,
We must do,
What is best for all of you,
In the factories,
In the homes,
Coal is burning,
That's your cue.

How can we stop
The fossil fuels
From being the thing
We always use?
CO2 is rising up,
Now can we stop it?

Jamie Owen (12)
d'Overbroeck's College: Leckford Place, Oxford

Silent Death

Animals' homes are being vandalised
So many are lying in the shivering leaves
There are more homeless animals than we've realised
Because of humans building houses or cutting their trees

A lot of species are dramatically dying
As fast as lightning they fall to the ground
Their homes destroyed and their food lacking
Some are extinct; they died without making a sound

We see absolutely amazing creatures
Venturing beautiful lands
All of them with wonderful features
Bang! They're gone; we killed them with our own hands.

Sandra Brinster-Martelloni (11)
d'Overbroeck's College: Leckford Place, Oxford

Teenagers

The teens are all hooded, that's what you think
They ruin the city, with cans of spray paint
They drink and do drugs, that's all they are
But stereotypes, that's all that it is

The media have portrayed us this way
Nobody knows, the good things that we do
If something goes wrong, where are the teens?
But stereotypes, that's all that it is

Feral and wild, that's what they say,
In certain situations that may be true
But who do you think wrote this, hey?
But stereotypes, that's all that it is

But actually we teens are not what you think
We don't do drugs and we do not drink
We're civilised people, unlike you think,
Because stereotypes, that's all that it is.

Tom Kennedy (13)
d'Overbroeck's College: Leckford Place, Oxford

Money

Society brings us
To spend and then fall;
People get money for 'most nothing at all.
A million pounds for kicking a ball,
A bit more perhaps – for singing a song,
A few words in the air,
And then it's all gone.
Injustice, unfair,
For some that are others –
For people that labour
Instead of just take,
- But money not favour
For those that need to feed,
Society brings us –
To spend outside our need.

Patrick Anderson (13)
d'Overbroeck's College: Leckford Place, Oxford

Animal Testing

Huge hands reach for me
Always in a cage with a lock and no key
Waiting for my next dose that could be the end of me
They take me away in the cold and dark

Poke me and prod me to make me sleep
Then I lay there without a peek
'Go away!' I yell but they can't understand me
But I'm helpless, helpless I say

Please, please stop this
Don't do this to me
I lie there in my cage locked with no key
I wake up to find I am no longer me

I feel pain, I feel shame, I have fallen insane
I scream inside and realised
They have taken my eye
Now I want to die.

Jonny Clayton (15)
d'Overbroeck's College: Leckford Place, Oxford

Rainforest

Thick, mossy grass and dead leaves cover the floor.
Colourful songbirds flap and squawk high above the canopy.
Tiny beetles of every colour scuttle across this damp, soggy ground.
Monkeys silently slip and slide through the trees.

The rainforest.

But it was all in my dreams.
There's no forest here now: no trees to be found.
Animals lying dead on the ground.
Stumps of trees every few metres, smog and smoke fill the air.
Lions, tigers, the biggest beasts of them all,
Now they are lying dead on the floor.
For they are no longer the biggest beasts here,
Now they are us.
The rainforest, now a vast, bare wasteland.

Natasha Dodwell-Adams (13)
d'Overbroeck's College: Leckford Place, Oxford

Equal Rights

Up down, up down that's how the line goes.
Could we really live without
The men in yellow coats?
We'd be overrun by rats,
With nowhere to put our trash.
However
A brain surgeon saved someone's life
But that's only one,
Meanwhile there are 59 million people left,
And what would happen to them
If all we had were rats
Scurrying around in their trash
Litter on the floor
While we keep providing more
And more
And more
And more!

Molly Smockum Owen (12)
d'Overbroeck's College: Leckford Place, Oxford

The Arctic And Pollution

The seals are thinner
The polar bears are hungrier
Why is it that they have to suffer?
For our selfishness
Why do we live in luxury and
They live in a mess?
The ice is thinner
The penguins have to live
Without their fish
Why won't people see sense
And give up this nonsense?
Slowly and slowly
The ice is melting
Now is the time
Get your recycle bins out
And end pollution so
Everyone spread this motion.

William Thieba (11)
d'Overbroeck's College: Leckford Place, Oxford

At 16

They'll let me run, jump, shoot and die by the knife,
But I won't vote now in this life.

They'll let me leave school,
But not choose who sets the rules.

They'll let me treat the ill,
But don't care about my views on the Healthcare Bill.

They'll take my tax,
But I can't give them the axe.

They'll give me welfare,
But I can't say if it's fair.

They'll let me get married,
But not choose who gets ferried.

They'll let me choose my life,
But not vote for the future.

Joshua Harris (13)
d'Overbroeck's College: Leckford Place, Oxford

Nothing Is Left

Burning tide, squalid sand,
Leaves gone, plants gone.
The rainforest has fallen
Screaming as it was cut.
Nothing is left.

The birds are gone;
Oil was more valuable.
You can't drink the water,
And the rain is acidic.
Nothing is left.

Many pelts lie on the floor;
Their owners don't need them anymore.
Europe's gone; too much pollution.
America's gone; too much radiation.
Nothing is left.

Simon Kent (13)
d'Overbroeck's College: Leckford Place, Oxford

Politics

Politics can be useful in everyday life, but I am here to show you the way to do things right.
Don't charge too much for taxes or the people will rebel.
In London last year the riots started but if the politicians treated people with respect
None of this would have started.
Parliament promised no extra fees for education
But look at us today, do I really need an explanation?
The high fees have caused people to strike
And if this fee wasn't there the public would be back to school and happier.
Now politics is good as well and this is why.
Parliaments have helped us out so there is no reason to cry.
They give us good things like clean roads and the NHS.
But they could sort out the rest of the mess.
You don't have to listen to me but if you do,
We can make this a better country for the young people of today.

Jack Dunstone (12)
d'Overbroeck's College: Leckford Place, Oxford

Chelsea FC

Chelsea has a soul like an archangel in Heaven,
She scores like a shiny shoe thanks to the eleven.
On the pitch, in the changing rooms, in the stands, on the sideline,
All the players revved up from this favourite team of mine.

Roaring Roberto on the sideline revving the players up,
Abramovich smiles like a child holding his first ever cup.
New boys Hazard and Oscar doing their part for the club,
Lampard and Terry, true legends, and also every one of the subs.

Sebastian des Forges (11)
Farleigh School, Andover

Destruction

The Twin Towers,
Standing tall,
Centre of attention,
Soaring above us all.

Mothers working happily,
Fathers counting cost,
Oblivious to the fact
That all would soon be lost.

Two planes have been hijacked,
Threatened with guns and knives,
Women and children are crying,
Husbands are calling their wives.

Pedestrians watch in disbelief,
As each structure is hit by a plane,
Chaos strikes as people run
Towards the towers, in vain.

The towers are collapsing,
There is debris all around,
People know there is no hope,
They start jumping to the ground.

Millions of lives were lost that day,
We keep them in our prayer,
We fixed all the things we could,
But broken hearts are beyond repair.

Annabel MacDonald-Smith (11)
Farleigh School, Andover

War

War has a temper like a child at school in the playground,
He hurts horses and is horrible to humans and pain is found.
On the flooded floor of trenches and No-Man's-Land,
All are laid low with guns in their hands.

Harry Ashley (12)
Farleigh School, Andover

The War

They came at night
To start the fight
Yes, they came to start the war.
Destruction cast
From the first blast
When they came to start the war.

Poor children cried
And good men died
When they came to start the war.
A woman screamed
So loud, it seemed
When they came to start the war.

Some lightning struck
A passing truck
When they came to start the war.
Then thunder boomed
Canons consumed
When they came to start the war.

It all was still
And quite a chill
When they came to end the war.

Sophie Hall-Smith (11)
Farleigh School, Andover

Great Britain

Great Britain has a puffed out chest like a proud lion.
He's historic and traditional.
From Land's End to John O'Groats and London to Cardiff,
Scotland to Dover and its big white cliff.

Great Britain baking from North to South,
Scrummy scones, sponges and chips stuffed into mouths,
Perfect places to go from Big Ben to Giant Causeway,
You can watch a game at Twickenham, Lords or even Wembley.

Freddie Bossi (11)
Farleigh School, Andover

An Unfair World

It's an unfair world where we live in
luxury and others live in hell.

It's an unfair world where we are all
healthy and others are ill.

It's an unfair world where we live in
houses and others on the ground.

It's an unfair world where we go to
school and others don't go anywhere at all.

It shouldn't be like this,
we need to make a change,
so others can have more and we can
have the same.

Let's all come together and help to make
a difference,
so poems like this don't have to be written.

Claudia Vyvyan
Farleigh School, Andover

Of Writing A Poem

Write a poem they said,
It'll be easy they said,
First to find a nice easy zone, then I've got to think *about the* tone,
And adding alliteration as smoothly as allowed,
Wouldn't be possible without some slap, pop, sound.
In case you haven't noticed I've been using rhyme,
And I have been using rhythm all the time,
You tell me to use assonance . . . please explain what that is?
I think I'm meant to write this poem, so it's none of your biz,
I try to work by all the rules and that is hard, so I
Know you'll agree that I ain't no bard,
I think I will use similes like a pro,
This poem is mine, so back off bro!

Anna Smith (12)
Glasgow Gaelic School, Glasgow

Refuge?

I have come to this country
With nothing,

I know nothing,

My father, murdered,
My mother left,
I had nothing.

I lived on the streets of Quito,
Ecuador.
When I was adopted
Malaria had struck,
I was taken to hospital,
It keeps coming back.

My new father said we had to leave
My new mother was shot,
We were next.

Our plane left for somewhere
I trusted it would be nice.
We landed in a place called Glasgow,
Would this be the beginning of a good life?
It's so cold here,
We sleep on a park bench,
We beg under a building.

Nobody cares about us
We are only rubbish.
Parents worry that their children will end up unemployed.
At least they have a family,
At least they have safety.

At least they have a life.

Samuel Dow (13)
Glasgow Gaelic School, Glasgow

Racism Poem

Just because our skin,
May not be the same,
Doesn't mean you can make fun of me,
Exclude me from your games.

Just because I'm black,
And just because you're white,
Doesn't make us all that different,
I have feelings too, alright?

All the names you shout at me,
They really hurt inside,
'Indian', 'Browny', 'Chocolate',
It hurts the way you talk of it.

'Muslim', 'Hindu', 'Sikh',
You call me a black freak,
How would you like it if I made fun of you for being white?
All the nasty comments swirling round your head at night.

Being bullied,
Is like being the odd one out,
No one hears me scream or shout,
If I run or if I cry,
You bully me more,
My question is why?

But now I don't care if you pick on me,
My skin is what defines me,
I am black and I am proud,
I don't care if you snigger or chatter,
It's what's inside that really does matter!

Eilidh Miller (13)
Glasgow Gaelic School, Glasgow

Drugs = Thugs

He walks down the street showing off the latest trends,
Music pumping through his earphones as he texts to his several friends.
Little did he know, his fun was coming to an end.

On the opposite side of the street a tough guy swaggers along,
His head wasn't in the right place; because he was off his face.

As he walks past the boy, with his gadgets hanging about,
He pushes him against the wall and doesn't hesitate to shout.

The boy gets a fright and loses his tight grip on his gadgets. The druggy smiles
with delight and takes the boy's gadgets and the boy knows not to put
up a fight.

The crack face walks away with a smile on his face knowing the gadgets will sell
and get him off his face.

Drugs are bad, they make you feel sad and they can even make you go mad.
Don't take drugs, don't take drugs, you'll end up turning into a thug.

Make the right choices,
Don't be a fool,
You don't have to take drugs to make you look 'cool'.

So take my advice – what I'm trying to say is true,
Don't take drugs or a few years down the line you most certainly won't be you.

Don't be daft just take the right path,
And stay away from drugs like crack,
But remember all drugs are just as bad.

Many people take them today,
but take my advice and stay away.
You'll have a bright future ahead, but if you take drugs in 20 years you'll be dead.

Donald Morrison (13)
Glasgow Gaelic School, Glasgow

Education Poem

Science, maths, history solving the mystery,
The education and federation,
Makes us angry with frustration.

Reading and writing,
Not drugs or fighting,
Dedication to my education
Keeping my future bright

Now is the time to get good grades,
So we don't turn out as maids,
Revision could give you a good job,
But if you lie around you're most likely to end up like a slob.

We're young with dreams,
Like being famous or being in a football team,
For now think about these things in your spare time,
And focus on your English rhyme.

School is fun in all different ways,
They are the most important days,
Your subjects may not be the best,
But that means working harder than the rest.

Further ahead it will come in handy,
Don't wait around eating candy,
Seven years in primary, six years in high school,
Don't fail your exams just to look cool.

Mairead MacLennan (12)
Glasgow Gaelic School, Glasgow

Snail Pace

Moving at a snail's pace
Leaving trails of slime all over the place
Eating fruit and moving slow
That's just how I like to roll!

When some people see me
They try to step on me
But others pick me up
And put me somewhere high up

As I sit on the ledge
Just above the hedge
A worried looking boy passes
And people are making glances

The boy starts running
And others following
Until he trips up
And gets beaten to a pulp

Why are some humans so cruel?
Yet others are so cool?
Can't everyone get along?
I guess I'm wrong . . .

Nicola Campbell (12)
Glasgow Gaelic School, Glasgow

It's Never Enough!

'Take a drink, take a drink,' said aw ma pals!
The first time wis disgusting but soon I liked the taste,
Then a buzz of drinking became my life, what a waste!

'Take a fag, take a fag,' said aw ma pals!
Puff! Choke! Cough! Man it's rank
Soon you're onto 20 a day and having to hit the bank.

'Take a hit, take some heroin,' said aw ma pals!
'It'll gie ya a good time, you'll no get hooked.'
So I tried it coz they're ma mates,
Now I'm an addict, the person everyone hates!

What age am I? What age am I?
I look seventeen when I'm only thirteen!
They can't tell me what age tae take a drink, a fag, some heroin!
Just know tae go doon this path you'd be chucking your life in the bin!

Now down the line in ten years time,
Look where I am noo, listen up this could be you
Buried six feet doon,
Rebekah Boyle gone too soon!

Rebekah Boyle (12)
Glasgow Gaelic School, Glasgow

Turtles Poem

Sea turtles, wild turtles, baby turtles, pet turtles,
Turtles, turtles, turtles, turtles,
Turtles, turtles, turtles.

They all have a shell,
But not a hotel,
It's always a house,
Unlike a mouse.

They eat snails and worms and insects too,
Sometimes they eat fish like you,
A lot of vegetarians in our sea,
Turtles are very cool can't you see.

One hundred years to live,
Under the sea,
I think I'd rather just be me,
To live that long under the sea,
Must be a nightmare or is it just me?

Alix Wardrope (13)
Glasgow Gaelic School, Glasgow

Environment Poem

If we keep going the way we are our world will not go very far.

We are cutting down trees but not for much longer we aren't making our world any stronger.

The world is heating up fast like a wind in the winter so if we don't stop soon we might have to live on the moon!

Broom, broom the chainsaw goes taking away the last of the trees.
Timber, timber, broom and crack all the limber pines are gone.
What will happen when we run out of trees we won't have any more green tea.

The icebergs are melting so sea levels are rising and the scientists are advising for us to save as much energy as we can so they can plan how to save our planet.

What if the time comes we haven't found a way, for not saving energy we will have to pay.

So if we don't stop this you can kiss the flowers goodbye.

Rory Connelly (13)
Glasgow Gaelic School, Glasgow

The Highwayman

The highwayman's eyes are as black as coal,
He rides along when you don't know,
He takes your money, purse and jewels
And makes you feel like a stupid fool.

He leaves a trail of blood beneath his feet,
If you stand up to him he'll make you back down in defeat.

He trots along the muddy path,
Then he'll kill you, then he'll laugh,
People say keep out of sight
Because he could be coming for you tonight.
The spirits of his victims walk beside him,
He is ever so grim.
So if you see a dark black shadow
Perched upon a big fearsome horse . . . run!

Kate Cheer (11)
Ifield Community College, Crawley

Broken Pieces

Life and death follow us daily,
While hate and love spiral through the world,
A ship that crashes, 'mid its sailing,
Destroying lives that have not uncurled.
The good, bad, terrible and worse
Like the last dying breath
Of a mother's sweet first.

Lives that we lost,
Lives that were not found,
Lives that remain broken,
While others rot in the ground,
Mistakes not being taken,
The guilty refusing the blame,
Ambitions are breaking, while
We're all chasing the fame.

The who's who and did what's,
The when, where's and how's
Role models proving believers wrong.
Leaving all originality to drown.

Bringing up an act,
Not being true to themselves,
As we all watch, knowing
That the truth will come out.
That their lives will follow the course,
All set before us,
Whether it be death, hate or love,
We will all suffer the torment.

Because there is only so far in life,
That we can pretend,
That the courage within us . . .
Will never end.

Emily Ann Roberts (16)
Ifield Community College, Crawley

Joey's First Experience Of War

We stood in the desolate countryside, trembling.
Mist hung over the field as if hiding some nightmarish secret.
The clouds were the colour of bruises.
Through the mist, shadows of all shapes and sizes could be seen.
Everyone knew a fight was about to begin,
Even though the enemy was invisible,
We knew they were there, you could hear them.
What was I doing here?
What were we all doing here?

I froze with fear,
The time was near.
A shiver of terror shook my body,
War was not my favourite hobby!
No sweet words of comfort could calm me down.
For a moment there was silence . . . not a sound.
I could taste the tension thick in the air,
I could smell the depression that I could not bear.
The swords were drawn,
Put on a brave face we had sworn.
The commands were made,
Then with those devilish blades,
We rode towards death.

The throbbing of my heart was almost as loud as the pounding of hooves.
The guns began to fire fast,
I dodged at every blast.
Never have I heard such ear-piercing screams,
Not even in my endless dreams.
Bang! Another life lost,
Bang! Where's my rider?
This could have gone a lot kinder.
I ran, no way but forward, a mindless bullet.
It could not be, could it?
He didn't deserve it!
It wasn't worth it!
I left him, wrapped in a blanket of agonising pain,
I knew it was wrong, but what could I do? This war was insane!

After that it went by in a blur, so quick.
I felt so sick.
I entered the crowd of tall, towering trees, their arms waving me on.

I was safe, danger was gone.
Yet just one look,
Was all it took,
For a heart-wrenching feeling to creep over me,
With all the horrors of war I could now see in front of me.
It was once a battlefield, now a graveyard.
They were once living, now dead.

Keely Holland (12)
Ifield Community College, Crawley

Scarred Heart Of A War Horse

Heart tightened, hooves shivered, it was time,
Jewel amongst a crown, I stood gallant.
Mighty kings blanketed by the filthy, ragged rugs of war.
Sunlight of battle seared my skin.
This was the cloud, the thunder echoing my life. This was war.

Proud battle cry, more a helpless child's screech,
My life was put into perspective, no time to ponder.
Soldiers' eyes flooded with the toxic sorrows of war.
We fell, oh we fell . . . Unmerciless was Death's touch.
Dented, my soul, my heart, my spirit were.
Yet how was I still standing, when so many were falling?

Swords cowered away, their glimmer didn't prevail over this forever darkness,
They were gone, he was gone, I ride alone.
Burn of goodbye nothing compared to death. We know not their fate.
Souls imprisoned in the spiked, blood-drenched cage that be war.
He had jailed their dignity, and oh were the hell fire ravenous for it!

Fallen as soldiers of war, risen as heroes of humanity,
Leaving their bloody footprints in the sands of time.
No matter how many captured, they lay injured in our hearts.
Now my eyes are heavy with the weights of war
And they are burdened with debt we must fight for.
So daren't forget this,
For it's a tale from a scarred heart of a war horse.

Sara Moufeed (12)
Ifield Community College, Crawley

Life Of A Raindrop

Ticka-tocker-tippa
crushing onto the floor
say goodbye before I
leave

Ticka-tocker-tippa
my daily routine
get the world wet
all year long

Ticka-tocker-tippa
my daily routine
one day here
next day gone
where have I
gone?

Tired of this life
always a routine

Had I chosen the
wrong life of a
raindrop?
Ticka-tocker-tippa

Syed Hajid Hussain (12)
Ifield Community College, Crawley

The End

Goodbye
I will remember you
You might be gone
And your memories lost
But I will remember you.

You've been in my life
For a great deal of time
There have been ups and downs
But in the end it does not matter
What matters most is the time I have spent with you.

Matthew Graves (12)
Ifield Community College, Crawley

My War Experience

I saw the soldiers,
And knew what was to be done,
I saw Captain Nicholls' sword,
But soon he was gone.

I carried on galloping,
Only because there was nowhere to go,
I scattered them all,
And now I was a hero.

I met my new rider,
He reminded me of Albert,
He obviously wasn't,
Trooper Warren was his name.

Topthorn spoke to me every day,
He gave me comfort and confidence,
Even Captain Stewart,
They looked after me terribly well.

Who was I?
How did I get here?
I was only a farm horse,
A few days ago.

Manan Vaidya (12)
Ifield Community College, Crawley

The Highwayman

The highwayman is evil.
He will come to you.
If you do bad things,
He might even have a gang of other highwaymen and robbers.
Highwaymen are scary.
'Who will we go to?'
A policeman or the vicar?
A very silly man to go to.
The highwayman makes a terrible mistake.
Nooo! That's the path he took!

Stephanie Stevens (11)
Ifield Community College, Crawley

The War Horse

Struck with fear, I nervously walked on.
I could feel the tense soldiers in my troop.
The light, refreshing breeze, my only comfort.
The gentle neigh of my colleague, telling me it was time.
Crash!
I could hear the enemy ahead.
Suddenly, Bang!
Gunshots filled the air.
I was a lion, bravely dodging bullets.
Turning around, I saw the bodies of brave men gently thud on the ground
Utter torture.
They lay lifeless.
Then, overcome with courage, I went from trot to canter, from canter to gallop,
thoughts flooded my mind of my life,
knowing I had to overcome this war.
Like a cheetah, I galloped the safest way possible,
my life my main priority.
I stopped!
My heart beating 100 beats a second.
Silence.
I had survived!

Annie Jane O'Rourke (12)
Ifield Community College, Crawley

The Dread Of Battle

We arrived, the cry of battle caught my ears and we charged into the fight,
weapons raised by both sides.
Blood being spilled across the battlefield.
Each bullet shot, taking one human life.
I heard the battle cries coming from my rider and then they stopped.
His sword on the floor beside his desecrated and disrespected corpse,
I turned to see him bathing in the blood of many men including his own.
I charged at the enemy like a bull kicking,
shoving and stomping on all who stood in my way,
and during my charge my mind was full of only one thing.

A life for a life.

John Garner (12)
Ifield Community College, Crawley

Captain Nicholls' Final Stand

Out from the covering canopy of the lofty trees,
Adrenaline coursing through my veins as I settled into a high tension rhythm.
Clip-clop, clip-clop,
I was but a bee amongst a swarm,
A cub amongst a pride.

Every stallion to rider knew we may not make it,
Though we were driven by an invisible force,
The wind blowing her soft cool breeze against my chestnut locks
And then it started.

Bang! Bang! Bang!
Sounded as though hundreds of balloons were popping in the area started,
As horses and men alike fell harshly to the cold, dead earth,
Various smells and a feeling of fear gripped me, shaking me into a frenzy.

I called in desperation but no response,
What was happening?
The soft hands guiding me fell slack,
My soft, gentle rider Captain Nicholls.

Now motionless and empty upon the ground,
The ghost of his final smile clinging to his features.

Nicole Buckley (12)
Ifield Community College, Crawley

The Highwayman

As the highwayman came riding,
Everyone stopped and stared,
Not only did he chuckle,
But strokes his long dark hair,
As he rides through the twinkling sun,
Everyone caught a glimpse of his golden gun.
He rides past, he aims,
He plays his stupid games,
He tilts his French hat,
Gleams at you with his eyes like a cat,
But that's just the highwayman for you.

Jodie Barker (11)
Ifield Community College, Crawley

The Battle

The horses ran
The rifles raised
The swords were drawn at last
The deadly noise of guns and war
Filled the fiery air
The crash and clap of all the noise
Sent me in a spin
My rider gone
A wounded leg
Was it over yet?
The guns they smiled
A grimacing grin and shot
Down another horse.
Was it a friend or foe?
I really didn't know,
But then a grassy field,
A nice warm bed of hay
I finally rested
My tired head.
It was over now.

Mia Blackman (12)
Ifield Community College, Crawley

Born To Run

Only five months old,
A strong old colt,
Sold off at an auction
For only three guineas,
Ripped away from my mother,
She was sold within minutes,
A fine old horse,
I went soon after,
But I found a spiffing new partner,
Albert was his name,
He trained me and loved me,
Now I'm ready.

Lewis Freeston (12)
Ifield Community College, Crawley

Joey's Final Days

Albert was riding me, morning, noon and night
This kindness to me was a shocking fright
Stroking, patting, feeding and grooming
My morale in life is greatly booming
Running through the forests
The trees hovering over us
Like hawks stalking their prey.

Splashing through streams
Jumping over gates
When Albert rode me he forgot all his traits
Until one morning I had a spook
Something in the bush went *te-aa-croock!*
It was a ginormous snake bigger than me
Looking in my eyes you see
I began to run and then I realised
My body started to paralyse
I turned and galloped back and sure enough
There was Albert, lying flat on his back.

Ashley Gregory (12)
Ifield Community College, Crawley

The Highwayman

He's a mysterious, cold-blooded animal,
With a heart as black as coal,
A meanful smile he wears,
Even though he might seem nice,
Under the dark cloth skin lies
A devil in human disguise.

Although he might seem alright,
His life a handful of lightning,
Striking down on you, it's so frightening,
A devil in human disguise.

Who knows, you might not awaken,
On your cold blood it's not mistaken,
For you, you will not survive.

Craig Hicklin (11)
Ifield Community College, Crawley

My War Experience

I missed Albert,
I missed the farm,
I missed Old Zoey,
I missed the routine.
We all thought war would be an exciting experience,
But as soon as I set foot on the battlefield,
Fear took over my entire body,
From head to hooves – I was suddenly terrified,
Though I had to stay concentrated and determined,
A gun fired and we were suddenly in action,
I ran and ran,
People dropping like flies around me,
I didn't stop,
I couldn't risk it,
I had to keep galloping on,
Where was I? What was I doing?
A weight suddenly lifted off my back
And all final remains of hope were lost . . .

Amber Jane Warrell (12)
Ifield Community College, Crawley

The Fault In Our Stars

I remember, when I was nine,
We looked at the stars that shone above our old home town,
We watched, almost dazed, as they gleamed gold and silver,
We whispered silent secrets that only those stars could hear,
But after you left I cried a single tear,
To think you left me here.

You went and left to be with her because you thought I wasn't good enough,
and now you're standing here on the same starry night,
Wishing you hadn't pushed your luck,
but that's the fault in our stars,
We may have crossed once, but that's the way destiny goes,
on a dusty moonlit road,
To a never-ending eternity of in and out pain,
Life is like that, but I will never love again.

Jessica Olim Félix (13)
Ifield Community College, Crawley

Highwayman

A mysterious man
Goes round in his clan,
He committed a crime,
We need to find him in a short time.

He rides a horse,
Doing an assault course,
His done his killing,
It was thrilling.

He must be related to the Devil,
Because he's quite a rebel,
He isn't comfortable,
He's too horrible.

Please help me,
He might be hiding behind a tree,
The highwayman,
In his clan.

Jay McGee (11)
Ifield Community College, Crawley

On The Battlefield

Where was Albert and everything I knew?
I was left only with my rider's company,
As my rider slowly pulled out his heavy sword,
I heard the thunder of guns sounding violently.

The trees were smiling nervously as we galloped by to wish us luck,
When I got scared, a gentle hand stroked my nose,
But the death rattle of machine guns broke the silence,
It was as if we had met our match.

When it came to the autumn,
The frost was upon us,
We could always hear a jingling harness,
For the terror in our eyes grew worse by the minute,
We were lost in the dark, all alone.

Aysha Mehmood (12)
Ifield Community College, Crawley

Who Am I?

I only hunt at night
With talons as sharp as could be
I only roam the wood so fast
So I can find my tea
It might just be worms
But that's what makes, me, me.

I roam the night sky
Sometimes I want to fly away
Seems as I have no family
There's nothing there for me.

I only hunt at night,
With talons as sharp as could be.
I only roam the wood so fast
So I can find my tea.
It might just be worms
But that's what makes me, me.

Luke Malin (12)
Ifield Community College, Crawley

War Horse

W inters were hard, treacherous and cold which rattled my teeth.
A wkward, annoying and awful, my training was long, hard and miserable.
R iding up the hills the whistle intimidated me as I tried my best to
remain with old Zoey.

H undreds of miles stared ahead of me but the hands gripped tight
with no sign of letting go.
O nwards we travelled but I'd never feel a thwack make contact to my
thighs thus Albert would gently encourage me.
R embering how hard and bitter the winter was, my heart transformed into gold
as I felt spring slowly appear.
S o warm and tasty, Albert always finished my training with some oats but . . .

E ventually war was announced, was I going to be a war horse?

Jade Dancaster (12)
Ifield Community College, Crawley

Goodbye Highwayman!

He is a dark and gloomy fellow,
He is a sneaky and crafty fellow,
He is the highwayman and he will pay,
He will pay the price of justice!

He has lost lives,
He has cost money
And now he will pay,
He will pay the price of justice!

He rides like a king,
But he is not!
He dresses like a king,
But he is not!
He thinks he is a king,
But he is not!

That's why the highwayman will be stopped.

George Smith (11)
Ifield Community College, Crawley

The Highwayman

T ears of cold, dark blood run down his face,
H is horse goes clipperty-clop down the mysterious lanes,
E *eahh!* screams his innocent prey,

H e is too ghastly to look at as you could be his next victim,
I nnocent people's ruby-red blood stain the rocky floor,
G hosts follow him to try to scare his curse away,
H aunted shadows scream to hear the clip-clop of his horse,
W illiam; the name of his horse,
A lthough people are out to get him,
Y elling through the country,
M any people frightened of him,
A s his body lurks through the shadows,
N obody knows where he is.

Ben Wright (11)
Ifield Community College, Crawley

Stars

High in the sky,
Way beyond the clouds,
Little lights flicker all around.

I see them there,
But only at night,
They are miles away but seem so bright.

They have their own world,
Where they are free,
And never controlled unlike me.

Stars are like angels,
Looking down on us,
Keeping safe as they must.

Jade Belbin (13)
Ifield Community College, Crawley

The Highwayman

Evil, ghastly and deadly,
Yes, the highwayman.

Sneakily hiding the golden gun,
He only leaves a tiny trail,
Of smelly, rotten flesh and death.

His big black cap flaps over his eyes,
To hide his cunning disguise.
A long velvet robe strapped over his shoulders,
His thighs are as big as boulders.

Oh what a killer the highwayman is,
Just wait till us, the police, catch you
And end your murders!

Lee Cooper (11)
Ifield Community College, Crawley

The Highwayman

People say he's heroic,
But is this really true?
He's an evil criminal,
He may be coming for you!

He goes round towns,
Killing with no regret,
Shooting, punching, stabbing!
His target is set!

So if you see the highwayman,
Run for your life!
Or you can go up to him
And get stabbed by a knife!

Ethan Turner (11)
Ifield Community College, Crawley

The Highwayman

The highwayman is a devil,
He sneaks through the night,
He's a beast that's evil,
As he stalks through the night.

The highwayman's a tiger,
A violent, vicious monster,
That takes you out like a sniper,
As he stalks through the night.

With his golden gun
And his rapier slasher,
Killing people, he feels it's fun,
As he stretches out of sight.

Alex Case (11)
Ifield Community College, Crawley

The Highwayman

H e is a devil in human form.
I s he a local villager?
G hostly he is, like the sound of chainsaws.
H e rides into the mist.
W hen leaving his victims screaming,
A deathly trail he leaves behind him,
Y ou better close your eyes, as things are getting ugly.
M ay he be punished, for all he has done,
A whistle he makes, acting ever so innocent.
N ever fall for his tricks, as you will be next, beware I say,
beware – all is cursed!

Chloe Coaker (12)
Ifield Community College, Crawley

The Highwayman

The highwayman is wrong,
He hasn't got no heart,
He has a girlfriend,
He'll probably kill her too!

He may look really sweet,
Doesn't mean he is.

He rides his horse like he don't care!
A heart of stone and a brain of steel.
He may look nice on the outside
But he has no feelings on the inside.

Harley Austin (11)
Ifield Community College, Crawley

Life

Life is like a game of cards,
It represents determinism,
But the way you play your life,
Is free will.

Some say if you are good in one
life you are rewarded in the next,
but is there a next?
Or are you another card in the devil's deck.

Some people's lives are like a chameleon
they would change themselves just to fit in.

Rakshit Jirjadhun (12)
Ifield Community College, Crawley

The Highwayman

H e has a devilish personality
I n a dark coat he stands
G uy with a golden gun
H e has a mysterious look on his face
W hen you see him you must run
A nd hide
Y ellow holster to keep his gun
M urderer
A n evil person killing everyone
N ever mess with the highwayman.

Joe McElderry (11)
Ifield Community College, Crawley

My Cousins

In summer they are active.
In autumn they are captive.
In spring they are like little fires.
In winter they are tired.
In every season they are ready for another day of having fun.

Shanae Nayee (12)
Ifield Community College, Crawley

The Highwayman

H ighwayman is evil.
I 'd hate to say, but his next victim could be you!
G irls, boys, he don't care, whoever he sees he will kill!
H is heart is as black as coal.
W ho will be his next victim? Nobody knows.
A messed up man, an evil man.
Y ou, me, could be killed, he takes your money and your life.
M urderer! That's what he is.
A n evil villain, evil man, there's no other way to describe him.
N obody knows who he really is.

Tierney Cooke (11)
Ifield Community College, Crawley

Stars

S o pretty in the night sky
T winkling around
A ll around us lighting our path up
R otating the Earth they will follow
S himmering like crystals

Oh star I love
Oh star I do
Shine upon me
Light up my way.

Rebecca Waller (12)
Ifield Community College, Crawley

When I Lie On My Bed

When I lie on my bed I think of your
luscious, golden, blonde, yummy hair!
When I lie on my bed I think of your
sweetest conversations!
When I lie on my bed I think *are you my shining star?*
When I lie on my bed I think *naah you'll just be another shooting star!*

Aksa Ahmad (12)
Ifield Community College, Crawley

Ghastly And Evil

Ghastly and evil, the highwayman rides his
outstanding horse through the dark, dark night.

Ghastly and evil, you hear the staggering
hooves of the horse galloping rapidly.

Ghastly and evil, the shimmering moon beams down
to the cold-hearted, devil-like criminal.

Ghastly and evil, the highwayman glares with
his measly eyes at his next murder.

Kieran Martin (11)
Ifield Community College, Crawley

Highwayman

In the dark village
A dark, mysterious soul is upon,
With his skin like the night's sky,
He rides all day and hunts all night.

His heart as black as coal,
Everyone wants him to die in a hole,
He's half devil,
So be careful of the dark rebel.

Shellby Jones (11)
Ifield Community College, Crawley

War Horse Acrostic Poem

W e had arrived,
A fter a long ride,
R ight into the battle, all

H ell broke loose,
O n my back no more,
R iding in the clouds,
S ir Captain Nicholls,
E nvies life itself.

Louis Perry (12)
Ifield Community College, Crawley

Escaping Death

He could hear the beating of her heart.
He could already taste the thick red liquid flowing through her veins.
His eyes turned a deadly shade of red.
He smiled at her, showing a full set of pearly white teeth,
as her strode towards her.
A tall spotlight on her, picking her out of the shadows.
Eventually he reached her and with an almighty push, he was dust.
A man walked up to her and said, 'You can't escape death.'

Hannah Allessendro-Pearse (13)
Ifield Community College, Crawley

The Afterlife

When I die the clocks stop ticking
I look back and think to myself
What could I have done to be better
Take back all the sins and turn back?

I want to go back, but I
Simply can't because this is
The afterlife.

Oliver Loughton (12)
Ifield Community College, Crawley

The Debate

They sat round the table and began their debate
Shakespeare stood up, in an agitated state
'We must decide now whose work is the best
Who wrote the literature that's above all the rest?'
Said Charlotte, 'Tis me, for Jane is iconic.'
Replied Emily, 'Should you win, it would be highly ironic
For your work is dull, whereas mine's full of madness.'
'And mine's overshadowed,' whispered Anne with great sadness.
Said Barrie, 'Kids love me, I created Peter Pan.'
Announced Burgess, 'I'm daring, my book received a ban.'
'For good reason,' called voices, 'Your novel was gruesome.'
'Ours was much better,' declared the Grimm twosome.
'But mine's full of magic, it has trees that can walk.'
Replied Carroll to Tolkien, 'But could your caterpillars talk?'
Stated Kerouac, 'My novel is by far the best ride.'
'Does yours though,' asked Austen, 'have both prejudice and pride?'
Said Salinger, 'None could beat The Catcher in the Rye.'
'Yet no narrative but mine involves Big Brother's watchful eye.'
Orwell seemed smug, until Stoker said,
'True, but your novel lacks the living dead.'
'Mine has that too!' exclaimed Angela Carter.
'But his soul to the Devil my protagonist does barter.'
This was said by Marlowe but laughed at by Alcott,
'You think he's better than Jo? Chris dear, I think not.'
'May I make a point?' said Tolstoy, before Marlowe's retort.
'Fine then,' said Hemmingway, 'but this time, keep it short.'
'I have heard of a novel, which appears quite unique.'
Cried the others, 'Who wrote it? Come on Leo, speak!'
'She's called E L James and people do say
There's no greater novel than Fifty Shades of Grey.'

Grace Garside (17)
Loreto Grammar School, Altrincham

Soldier

They stay up all night,
Just waiting for the fight,
They stay up all night,
I will make sure I hold you tight,
Please stay alive.

They cry all day,
Not sure they will make it all the way,
They cry all day,
They're not happy to pay,
Please stay alive.

They live for justice,
And are keen for this,
They live for justice,
And need this,
Please stay alive.

They keep us safe,
No matter the pace,
They keep us safe,
No matter what they face,
Please stay alive.

Believe me this is all true, the sleepless nights,
The crying all day, the justice they won't get
And the bit about keeping us safe,
So if you hear anything bad or just happen to walk by
And see a soldier, pay some gratitude,
They have saved your life.

Sian Louise Webb (12)
Mill Chase Community College, Bordon

Africa!

Perfection, glow of the rich sunshine,
Charming colours filled silent landscape,
The life blossomed and reflected adoration,
Savage animals of the peaceful wilderness.

Marcia Scaife (13)
Mill Chase Community College, Bordon

Ice Cream!

On a bright and sunny day,
an ice cream cart came to life,
selling ice cream all the way,
flavours that melted from ice.

Chocolate, vanilla and strawberry,
there are more flavours to go,
like caramel and blueberry,
who could ever say no?

As cold as the winter,
as wet the rain,
perfect for a sprinter,
before they run again.

As the sun goes in,
ice cream never dies,
it is eaten as pudding,
just like apple pies.

Just one scoop would make my day,
or maybe a few more,
look at all this ice cream, hip hip hooray,
it's the ice cream I adore.

Ice cream, ice cream what a cool sensation,
the flavours give me a kick,
tasty and nice in any combination,
heaven till the very last lick.

Kaitlyn Pool (12)
Mill Chase Community College, Bordon

Paradise Ends

Tigers dream of jungles
No more. The sea weeps,
The dead have nothing.
Paradise bereft of oceans,
Earth's water's gone.
Whales are wailing.

Drew Choularton (13)
Mill Chase Community College, Bordon

Trapped

Every one of them didn't care,
Of the pain that I had to bear.
The cruel tricks were the same,
They thought it was a game.

Why couldn't they see?
The aching within me.
I saw their darkness,
Without it they were powerless.

Every one of them didn't care,
Of the pain that I had to bear.
The cruel tricks were the same,
They thought it was a game.

Trapping me in a cage,
That filled me with rage.
I felt their ugliness,
It made me weak.

Every one of them didn't care,
Of the pain that I had to bear.
The cruel tricks were the same,
They thought it was a game.

I didn't feel any hope,
How did I cope?
They fed on fear,
It gave them victory.

Every one of them didn't care,
Of the pain that I had to bear.
The cruel tricks were the same,
They thought it was a game.

Everything was gone,
I was done.
I smelt their eagerness
To rip me apart.

Every one of them didn't care,
Of the pain that I had to bear.
The cruel tricks were the same,
They thought it was a game.
But now they feel shame,
Of their cruel little game.

Nasima Hussain (13)
Mill Chase Community College, Bordon

Child Abuse

As she whipped her
and shouted at her,
she cried and screamed.

As I stared into the little girl's
swollen and black eyes, I wished
that I could save her. But I am
just a memory and can't help in any way
to save the child.

She was thrown and strangled I had
to do something. So I closed my
eyes and the world went black, just
then the world went back to normal.
The girl was fine. No swollen, black eyes.
Her mum was making dinner
and loved her foster daughter
so much.

I wish I could never see the past
again but now she's fostered with a
lovely, new and caring mum, making
dinner as we speak, using the ingredients
of love and care. The other mum has been
handled with and is never to be
heard of again.

The old mum was imprisoned and
treated so brutally it's good she's hurt
because she was bad to the people.

Saffron Small (12)
Mill Chase Community College, Bordon

Dreaming Of Morning

Everyone was sleeping,
Not a single word was said.
In every house, silence
No sort of sound was made.

Snow fell down, peacefully,
As quiet as a mouse,
Covering everything with a white, fluffy blanket
And also every house.

No one was awake,
Everyone was asleep,
Except for one little girl
Who was filled with excitement.

Creeping down her wooden stairs,
A creak with every step,
Running to the window,
Opening the curtains, tore.

Staring through the window,
Emerald-green eyes glistened
As the sparkling snow slowed down,
More footsteps heard, listen!

Running up the staircase,
Running to her bed
Just before her parents saw,
Shaking excitement and adventure
From her imaginative little head.

Lara Chinn (13)
Mill Chase Community College, Bordon

Why?

'Come tonight,'
He sang to the stars and her.
The magic love blossomed,
A beautiful dream coming true,
Bringing joy and happiness,
Knowing they could be together day after day,
Living life, having fun to the maximum.

Broken laughter,
Music silenced.
Bones shattered, glass smashed,
His body as cold as ice,
Metal twisted, rubble everywhere,
A voice still called out.
Just one call too many
Was all it took,
To turn sparkling, tender eyes
To melancholy tears.

She never stopped believing
Hoping, dreaming
That one day
The passion they had
Would lead them out of the labyrinth of life and loss,
Together again,
Forever.

Lauren Cross (13)
Mill Chase Community College, Bordon

Cars On The Road

As the car starts moving,
In a car like a stomach,
The killing fuel inside starts brewing,
Like a disease about to be coughed all over.

The world starts to die from huge pain,
And the raving and horrible ranting starts again,
No more snow, sun or rain,
No more peaceful weather in a world full of hatred.

Now just dreading tornadoes, hurricanes,
Crashing down like tremendous boulders,
As powerful as the big bang, bigger than the entire universe,
Humans now must wish for great things.

They speak more of the petrifying putrid devil,
As he strikes he says, 'It has come'
The world must end like a man shot in the heart,
The clock stops ticking, the world stops turning . . .

If cars were abandoned,
The sun would shine and give us light,
And terrible weather would for certain go away,
More good weather will give us hope and spirit.

Jordan Plant (12)
Mill Chase Community College, Bordon

Hidden Evils

Purity of evil; life blossoms,
Comforting silence, illuminates ivory moonlight,
So savouring, summer's love ends,
Sorrow, sweet-blessings sickened,
Festered crimson heart and inked dreams bombarded,
In tragic faith let vengeance feast,
Still flight echoes and peacocks' chorus shades the shambles,
Glistening blood inclined to clot,
While stainless sun ripens savage
Consequently fortune distinguishes perpetuity to perpetrate.

Charlotte Cranmer (13)
Mill Chase Community College, Bordon

The Barrier Grief

Tropical fish swim
Through the coral reef,
Some apple-green,
As quick as a thief.

Waters are clear,
An azure blue,
The sun glints like diamonds
And sapphires too.

Divers will come,
Full of elation,
An underwater heaven,
With a unique population.

Treasures are hidden,
Some have been found,
Some lost forever,
Beneath rocky ground.

Fish bones and corpses,
Smother the bed,
Mankind has come,
And the fish are all dead.

Amelia Southern (14)
Mill Chase Community College, Bordon

Plebs

'Plebs'
There's nothing wrong with being a 'pleb'
'Plebs' work hardest for the country
They clean the streets and do the work
And lose out on good paying jobs
So don't abuse your government position
You might as well go live in a hole
For all the good it'll do.

Luke Skilton (13)
Mill Chase Community College, Bordon

Child Abuse

Crying out in the night,
Neighbours turn out their lights,
Screams and cries just to be heard,
No one says a single word.

They don't know what to do,
It's been happening since they were two,
If only we had some time to make it better,
But we don't so the tears make their cheeks get wetter.

Most of them wish they were never born,
They are kept up even at the crack of dawn,
They get told off if they yawn,
With their blood all over the lawn.

By morning they won't need to worry,
They will be in heaven in a hurry,
Away from those bullies,
We understand them fully.

They are happy to be away from Mum and Dad,
They treated them bad,
They aren't even sad.

Bethany Longman (13)
Mill Chase Community College, Bordon

The Scorpion

Eyes of emeralds
A cruel hybrid
The harbinger of doom
Weapons of icy poison
His head and lungs are so small
His bite is forever deadly
He kills his prey like a metallic monster
Clicked crimson pincers from its diminished prey
Eaten only by vultures
But in the form of corpses
Dead prey.

Luke Sykes (13)
Mill Chase Community College, Bordon

The Puss Needs A Fuss

She stares with her bright wide pearls fixed on me
Trying to lure me in
Little did I know she's been scavenging in a bin
I try to walk away but something pulls me back
The poor little thing's stuck in a raggedy sack
She lets out a cry
Too hard to ignore
Her ribs look like twigs
Not needed to be cut by a saw
I reach out my hands
Being very wary
But she seems to think, *scary, scary!*
I purse my lips and ask, 'Puss?'
All she needed was a little fuss
Pets are for life
Not to sacrifice
So think . . .
Think . . .
Pets have feelings too!

Francesca Smith (12)
Mill Chase Community College, Bordon

I Have A Dream . . .

I have a dream to be free
I hate doing all this hard work
Stupid men making me carry all of this
Up, down, up, down, all day long.

I have a dream to gallop through the wind
I hate being suffocated in this heat
My back hurts so much
I just want to live my life.

I have a dream to play with my friends
I hate having no one to canter with
I'm like a little billy with no friends
I dislike my life right now.

Laura Newens (12)
Mill Chase Community College, Bordon

Help This World

Yes there is pollution in the air
Oh my gosh, I just can't bear
Please help this world
Complete its shield
Come on, we can help

Just by recycling some bottles
We can fill up ten kettles
Just switch off the light
The sun is very bright
Come on, we can help

By saving trees
We can help the bees
If you save electricity
You would help our city
Yes we will help this Earth.

Bethany Benson (12)
Mill Chase Community College, Bordon

My Brother's Dream

Beloved sweetheart brother from childhood to adult
We have been friends. Through thick and thin
You stood by me, now I shall do the same.

Since your death I carried on
I'm finishing what you started.
The beautiful pebbles float down the river.
Blankets of ice cover the river in the cold winter.

I remember the day you stood next to me and said,
'I'm going to make this a river.'
You with your matted crimson beard.

You're dead now
But never worry, I always worked 'til dusk
As you wished, until your river was to perfection.

Lewis Brown (13)
Mill Chase Community College, Bordon

Poaching

Soon we will all be gone
We will be no more
Our fur used for warmth
Our bodies used for food
Out habitats torn down
What shall we do
Our skins used for carpets
Our heads mounted on walls
The paradise of our world
Crumbling down to the floor
Somehow, some way
We will get rid of them one day . . .

Luke Harrison (12)
Mill Chase Community College, Bordon

An Invasion On Earth

I am an alien who came down from space
To study some humans
And work on a case.

But I was surprised when I came down to see
Everyone stopped and stared at me.
They started to run, which I thought was silly
Then the army appeared and then tried to kill me.

They caught me again and again and again
As I kept getting free from their rather large den.
They ran me through tests
And put me in labs
And gave me injections
Oh how I hate jabs.

I sort of expected a wonderful time
But the things they did should be classed as a crime.
So now that I hate them I'll conquer their turf
For I am now planning . . . *an invasion of Earth!*

Paul Baillie (12)
Miltoncross Secondary School, Portsmouth

Child Abuse

Dear Diary,

It's like being in a cage
Nowhere to go
No one to tell

I watch it every day
That will be me soon
Listening to the yells

I can't avoid him forever
I can't even run away
The doors and windows are bolted

I'm listening now
It's petrifying
I hear a final scream

I open my door slowly
And I step outside
No more noise, I hope this isn't what it seems

I walk down the stairs
Slowly step by step
I walk to the front room door

He's sat on the sofa
A dull expression on his face
Head in hands

She is on her knees
Red velvet trickling from her head
On the floor she will land

He stops, looks up and stares at me
I guess it's my turn now
Goodbye diary, forever.

Hannah-Mae Stedman (12)
Miltoncross Secondary School, Portsmouth

Crime Bar One

There once was a guy from Newport
He was a criminal but he was caught
He was singing some jazz
While stealing a cat
And his goldfish was very distraught.

There once was a real sad guy
He lost something money can't buy
It wasn't his wife
But a butterfly knife
Which strangely, fell out of the sky.

There once was a guy called Steve
Who robbed some old guys leaves
The police locked him up
So they got a cup
And that is the story of Steve.

There once was a cat called Dan
He was a really, really good hit man
He killed seven guys
By using a pie
And driving a Babybel van.

There once was a postman called Pat
Who wanted a black and white cat
He had a red van
Filled full of Coke cans
They were stolen by a big bat.

Ashley Thompson (12)
Miltoncross Secondary School, Portsmouth

A Rose

A mazingly shining in the sun.

R eady to blossom up all in one.
O pening slowly and ready to blossom.
S lowly then dying and turning to fossil.
E very day is another day for a rose.

Charlie Wood (12)
Miltoncross Secondary School, Portsmouth

No To Racism

The girl who sits alone,
The one with the dark skin
And the dodgy phone.

She gets it a lot
The kicking and shoving
And put in headlocks

Being called black
And being left out
And never anything said back.

But enough is enough
An end must come
She'll act all tough

Hold back tears
Speak up for her rights
And hide all fears.

Tell the teachers
Get this sorted out.

See that girl who sits alone
The one with the dark skin
And dodgy phone.

Now she sits with friends
That help get through the day
Now her luck never ends.

Eden Leaney (12)
Miltoncross Secondary School, Portsmouth

Poetry

Poetry, poetry rhyming a little line.
Poetry, poetry writing all the time.
Poetry, poetry for the poetry games
Poetry, poetry that's the game
To win an iPad
Jordan's my name.

Jordan Smith (12)
Miltoncross Secondary School, Portsmouth

My Hero

A couple of long months ago,
I lost someone who meant the whole, wide world,
My beautiful nanny has gone,
Sadness doesn't explain my feelings,
Neither does my never-ending tears,
All I've got left over is pictures,
And unforgettable memories,
The day I found out she didn't make it,
My world went *bam!*
My heart stopped for a second,
Realising she'll never come back,
Crying myself to sleep,
Wanting that last hug and goodbye,
I got it in my amazing dream,
My nanny came to visit me!
I'm now very happy that she doesn't have to suffer,
Now she's in Heaven,
Looking down at me,
I hope she's very proud of me,
Like I am of her,
'Cause she's been the best nan for me,
I don't care if this isn't the best poem going,
But that's what I really feel,
I love you so much Nanny,
It's unbelievably unreal,
Rest in peace!

Nina Kinga Kaminska (12)
Miltoncross Secondary School, Portsmouth

Sister!

A sister is like a best friend,
Someone you can share your thoughts and feelings with,
But also may fall out with and argue,
They're always there for you,
Loving and caring each and every day,
I love my sister, I love her very much!

Georgia Tolson (12)
Miltoncross Secondary School, Portsmouth

Global Warming

Once there was ice on the poles
But now it's all covered in holes
The government's warning
It's not global warming
It turns out the culprit was moles

But we knew what they said was a lie
That the planet's beginning to fry
There's one thing to say
If we don't find a way
In years we might all burn and die

The trees and the plants they will burn
Leaving not even a fern
To even cockroach
Death will approach
Humans, will we ever learn?

The planet could be left singed
The humans, our legacy tinged
The skies full of smoke
The ground cracked and broke
And all cos on petrol we hinged.

Oscar Cherry (12)
Miltoncross Secondary School, Portsmouth

Life

L oving every step of life.
I n my future I won't have a wife, my choices
A re to stay single, maybe now and then I might
M ingle.

W hile making a pass to my life's end
O n the journey I'll need a friend,
R aging on in my head, as the years go
B y I'll be dead,
Y ou now understand why life's a fight
Now my poem's finished I'll say goodnight.

Liam Worby (12)
Miltoncross Secondary School, Portsmouth

The Tributes

The hunger games were not tame,
It was just people's thrill for the games.
The fighting, the clashing,
Even people slashing.

Tributes were dead,
Lying like a thread.
No matter the pain,
The blood would stain.

But there was me,
Taking a rest, drinking tea,
Then only one remains,
Playing the gory game.

Knowing I was done,
I thought about what I'd done,
It was rough,
I had, had enough.

Jake Miller (12)
Miltoncross Secondary School, Portsmouth

The Autumn Fox

He scampered and skittered through the browning, falling leaves of autumn
Along where the spiny hedgehogs sleep and snuffle for food.

The gleaming fiery red fur edged with crisp white,
Darts with grace, weaving around the towering trees.

The autumnal colours of leaves swirl, mix and tumble
In the golden peachy glow of sunrise in the woods

Leaves crunch under snow-white tipped paws.
Acorns and conkers litter the floor and moss adorns the ground like a
soft carpet.

Bushy tail bristling, his sleek body skips into the murky, damp warmth of the den.
All curled up the majestic magic fox falls far into a deep sleep

Until the next bitter night when breath hangs
Like ragged cloth in the pearly moonlight.

Jemma Hall (12)
Miltoncross Secondary School, Portsmouth

The Black Box

No one knows what's in it,
It will be a surprise.
It could be something dangerous,
Or something that flies.

The contents of the box
Are simply unknown.
It could be something creepy,
Chilling to the bone.

The items in the box,
Never to be found.
It could be something deadly,
From underneath the ground.

No one knows what's in it,
It will be a surprise.
Open up the lid,
And see it with your eyes.

Harrison Tupper (12)
Miltoncross Secondary School, Portsmouth

The Poetry Games

Time goes so fast.
Happiness when I win
Everyone in my district so happy
Peter determined to see me
One step and your life could be over
Everyone's depending on me
Trying to breathe whilst I'm homesick
Running away from my death
Year 2012 and already going to die
Gale is counting on me as I am him
As soon as I win I'm finding prim
Mum will always love me
Every district wants to win
So long in there but I have won.

Rosie Nancarrow (12)
Miltoncross Secondary School, Portsmouth

Day At The Beach

The sun on my face,
The sand in my toes,
The wind in my hair,
And the way my mum goes.

Put on some suncream,
Or else you'll get burnt
I've told you before,
I thought you had learnt.

When we must go,
I get so upset,
I ask to stay,
And see the sun set.

Sometimes we do,
Sometimes we don't,
Sometimes I'll ask to,
But sometimes I won't.

Shannon Ripley (12)
Miltoncross Secondary School, Portsmouth

Fighting

Fighting in the night
Someone could even die tonight
With no help from you, one even two
Raining now, you might even catch flu
Ding, ding, ding time for round three
Stop please, you are scaring me
Someone is down, what a shame
RIP to Mr Frame
Tap dancing in the rain
Like a frog leaping from drain to drain
Eyes staring from every corner
Another is on the floor
Do you want more?
You are breaking the law so *stop!*

Amelia Matthews (12)
Miltoncross Secondary School, Portsmouth

Fate Of The Future Youth

The clouds are coming,
Independence declared,
A million eyes crying,
Not one soul not scared,

The day is drawing,
Sea is getting rougher,
No love in the air now,
Sister or brother.

It is dark outside,
Teardrops in reflections.
Lined up in orders,
Every name mentioned.

Is it all a lie?
Is it all a truth?
Is this the fate of the future youth?

Ella Freeman (12)
Miltoncross Secondary School, Portsmouth

War

War is not what it looks like
You cannot really put it into words
Awake most of the bright days and cold nights
Shooting and killing men and women in herds
Spilling blood is not fun
Even if you're under the blazing sun
Watching your friends get shot
People next to you bleeding out
Seeing the enemy from afar seems like a dot
You know when someone's been hurt because there's a shout
Would you ever kill with the blood on your hands
Until the day when you climb the trench
When you get to no-man's-land
You're a dead man but at least you die away from the awful stench.

Nathan Dickens (12)
Miltoncross Secondary School, Portsmouth

Dark Clouds Are Coming . . .

Dark clouds are coming,
The once lively trees stoop down low
Green grass goes grey and animals begin to moan.

A fierce wind blows through,
Colour is sucked out of the town
Leaving nothing but a dreary grey,
Everybody is feeling down.

Dark clouds are coming,
Every smile morphs into a frown,
No one can escape it,
Nobody makes a sound.

Dark clouds are coming,
You cannot run,
The atmosphere is sinister,
Every child looks glum.

Kara Perryman (12)
Miltoncross Secondary School, Portsmouth

96 – Liverpool FC

What happened to the families is inexcusable
The FA tried to cover up
But the truth has just appeared.

For all those people that had died
Now they have got their justice
All us people that respect Liverpool FC
Are proud of all the things
That the families have been through.

We all love the way that Liverpool fans chant
'Justice for 96, justice for 96'
The Liverpool people have waited 23 years for this
And now it's the time they can feel
They have done justice for this tragedy.

Owen Baker (12)
Miltoncross Secondary School, Portsmouth

What Am I?

I am sly, I am slim
I am furry, I am fun

I have whiskers, not wings
I have a tail, not tentacles

I am lazy, I am little
I am cool, I am crazy

I have eyes, not eyebrows
I have ears, not unlike elves

I am who I am
I have nine lives

Can you guess who I am?

Chloe Bloxham (12)
Miltoncross Secondary School, Portsmouth

Bullying

You see that girl with bruises and black eyes
The one you called ugly,
She's suffering with her parents beating her.
You see that boy who you pick on
He came from far away
He is being racially abused.
You see those twins you laughed at
For being together all the time,
They suffer from being conjoined at birth.
These are just some of the signs of bullying,
This needs to stop,
No one should be treated differently.
Everyone is perfect in their own way.

Courtney Archer (12)
Miltoncross Secondary School, Portsmouth

Untitled

I hate homework, it wastes my time
I don't even get why it has to rhyme
You ruin my day
All I wanna do is go out and play!
You make my evenings bad
And I get yelled at and that makes me mad.
I like the weekend because there's no school
And I hate homework and that's all!
Sometimes I like the subject
But you really need to do some for food tech
I hate the history homework
And guess what?
I hate homework and now that's all!

Abbie Wilkinson (12)
Miltoncross Secondary School, Portsmouth

Equal Rights

E verybody deserves equal rights
Q uestion your actions
U nderstand their side
A ccept everyone
L ook after each other

R espect other people's differences
I believe in equal rights
G ood heart
H `ear my message
T hink of others
S pread the word.

Jez Brooks (12)
Miltoncross Secondary School, Portsmouth

The Poetry Games

P oems all about
O thers messing about
E veryone's trying to win
T eachers all around
R epeating the same thing
Y ou might

G et to win
A n iPod for the win
M aybe a Kindle too
E veryone's so confused
S o it might be you.

George O'Donnell (12)
Miltoncross Secondary School, Portsmouth

Imagine

Imagine if the trees were blue
Imagine if the sky was red
How can this be true?

Imagine if the houses were green
Imagine if the cars were yellow
I'm pretty sure this is a dream

Imagine if the earth was pink
Imagine if the water was orange
Well all you have to do is just think.

Bradley Arnott (12)
Miltoncross Secondary School, Portsmouth

Riot

Riots are in our town
They're not good for anyone
So we have to pay for it
Please don't riot
We don't like it.

Russell Musson (12)
Miltoncross Secondary School, Portsmouth

Food

I love food
Like cake, pizza and onion rings.
I like sour things
I like salty things
I like spicy things
I love Indian, Mexican
I love Italian, American
These are some of my favourite things.
But most of all the food I like is chicken wings.

George Taylor (12)
Miltoncross Secondary School, Portsmouth

Football

Football today is not exactly great.
I wish Danny Welbeck was my mate.
Nani over here, Cisse over there,
We ain't Chicago Bears.

There are great teams
Bad teams and truly average teams.
Messi, Aguero, Pineaar and Harris are all my faves.
If I was a manager I would pick them all.

Ben Harkness (12)
Miltoncross Secondary School, Portsmouth

A Bullying Poem

I hate this school,
And I hate you all.
You think you're all cool
To make me feel small.

You bully me
And make me feel like a pea
Why don't you just see
You're not cool to bully me.

Tom Cawte (12)
Miltoncross Secondary School, Portsmouth

Shopping

S etting out to go down town and I'm
H oping I'll find the perfect gift as I go in and
O ut of different shops, looking at the
P reposterous novelty items, wanting one, but I'm here for a
P resent to give to my extra picky friend but as
I expected, absolutely
N othing that's her taste, not one item except a box of chocolate that I eat as I
G o home.

Natasha Lavell-Smith (12)
Miltoncross Secondary School, Portsmouth

Untitled

The rain is pouring down, creating big puddles
Filling the cracks in the floor
Dripping down the window slowly
The sun comes out, here's a beautiful rainbow
Glowing in the blue sky.
In the cemetery my dad's grave is sitting there
In that cold, lonely place.
I love visiting it but I hate having to go.

Jake Major (13)
Miltoncross Secondary School, Portsmouth

Friends

Friends are made to be there when you're down,
Friends are made to eliminate your frown,
They always care,
They always share,
They always find a way to make you laugh,
Even if it is pretending to be . . . a giraffe,
So when you next meet up with your friend,
Tell them you want your friendship to never, ever end!

Ben Boden (12)
Miltoncross Secondary School, Portsmouth

South Park

South Park the best show on television.
Weekly mocking current events and celebrities alike
Charlie Sheen, Jennifer Lopez and even Jesus
Have been featured before
Even the Pope and the prophet Muhammad!
Constant controversy makes this show
And that's why I love it!

Max Ferrett (12)
Miltoncross Secondary School, Portsmouth

Drums

Drums are cool
Drums are sweet
Drums help you keep a beat
Play them when you're bored
You don't need a chord.

Daniel Brooks (12)
Miltoncross Secondary School, Portsmouth

A Mum!

A mum is like your closest friend
They are always there when you're down.
They help you through things,
And never let you down.

Macie Phipps (12)
Miltoncross Secondary School, Portsmouth

I'm An Old Spy From MI6

I'm an old spy from MI6
But don't tell anyone about this
Cos I'm undercover
Literally under the covers
Talking on my hovering phone
Chewing on a chicken bone

I remember the time in the Land of Wallami
The night I had eaten too much salami
I was taken prisoner because I knew the truth
About the plot of the exploding photo booths
As slick as a snake I snuck out of the place
Leaving in my haste a tube of poisonous toothpaste
(Actually it was intentionally placed)

As soon as I left the car I ran invisibly past Downing Street's cast of politicians
And grabbing a wad of snotty tissues
I deactivated the bomb with my bare hands and a barbed prong

But right now I'm just
An old spy from MI6
But don't tell anyone about this
Cos I'm undercover
Literally under the covers
Talking on my hovering phone
Chewing on a chicken bone.

Callum Manson-Visram (11)
Normanhurst School, Chingford

Across The Pitch

F ever pitch on the field
O vertime remains.
O nly one team can win
T he other team left in pain.
B all is flying through the air
A nother penalty.
L ast man shoots and scores the goal
L ifts the cup for all to see.

Hamza Khan (11)
Normanhurst School, Chingford

The Mermaid Tale

Under the sea is a whole new world,
Under the sea is the mermaid's pearls!

She keeps them in her golden treasure chest,
Which is in her bedroom, where she rests!

Her hair is as blonde as the golden sand
And her tail is as long as the whole wide land

It's scaly and as blue as the sea,
It sparkles and glistens just like me!

I'm a little fishy, my name is Mearl,
I'm the guard of the mermaid's pearls!

Working for the mermaid is a good job,
As long as I avoid the fishing rod!

One lovely calm day,
A handsome merman came to say,

'You're the most beautiful mermaid I've ever seen,
Why don't you come and live with me?'

The mermaid packed her bag and pearls,
And over her shoulder, she tossed her curls,

Then the mermaid and merman swam away
And that's the end of my story today.

Annabelle Aiken (12)
Normanhurst School, Chingford

Who Am I?

Don't worry what other people may say
Or the price you have to pay.
Skinny, fat, big or small
It doesn't matter if you're cool.

It doesn't matter if you're black or white
If you're a baker, butcher or a knight
All that matters is that you're you,
Unique, special and see every day through.

Michael McCann (12)
Normanhurst School, Chingford

Spring

Spring is a new born season,

To Spring, Winter is her older brother
Her children are the grass,
The earth and the flowers
That have just opened their buds
From the cold.

Daffodils blooming,
Nodding in the warm breeze,
Their sweet scent
Enveloping the countryside
Where the grass waves to them.

Rabbits popping their brown velvet heads
From their bank of burrows,
Whiskers twitching.
The golden sun reflects
Thousands of buttercups.

Wood anemones carpet the woodland.
Pure white stars.
The sunlight dappled
Through emerald leaves.
Forget-me-nots being picked
By friends.

Maya Simms (11)
Normanhurst School, Chingford

The Glorious Game

Listen to the roar, chants and cheers
Crowds in the terraces
Some hoot, some jeer

Old Trafford, Stamford Bridge and the Emirates Stadium
Teams arrive to play and all with ambitions
Come and play in these revered places
See world class goals, history in the making

Famous players that have children in awe
Enter the ground to wow us all
Zizou, the king of the glorious game
His talent unmatched, his personality the same

Manchester United my favourite team
The Premier League is where you'll be seen
Rio, Rooney and Van Persie
Their skill outstanding
How they amaze me

Trophies for the taking
May the best team win
Big pay cheques awaiting
Let the match begin.

Bilal Farooqui (12)
Normanhurst School, Chingford

The World's Worst Fears

I look around
I saw the tree cry
I felt the ground shiver in fear
Rain started to show its face
The world wasn't crying but dying
And we were killing it
We were killing the world with our
Gas and smoke
We were killing it with our factories
And soon all of Earth will have silence.

Harrison Peeling (11)
Normanhurst School, Chingford

Our Day Of School

Twins, we always fight
We don't want to go to bed at night.

In the morning we wake up with a sleepy head,
And our mum brings us breakfast in bed.

We brush our teeth and get dressed,
We're always rushing which makes us stressed.

We are in the car, we are running late,
Now we are rushing towards the school gate.

We get to the gate,
And we separate.

We go from class to class,
And every time we seem to pass.

Now we are lining up for lunch,
In a queue ready to munch.

Now I'm back in class,
Wishing time would pass.

As we leave the school gates,
We say goodbye to our mates.

Taylor Bennett (12)
Normanhurst School, Chingford

Night

There is magic in the night
But never magic in the light.
This magic is made by elves
Who swing shelf by shelf and make great spells.
These elves go two by two and never meet at the zoo;
The zoo is not a good place to meet
Elves are made of fine meat.
There is magic in the night
But never magic in the light.
This magic is made by elves
Who swing shelf by shelf and make great spells.

Sarah Clark (12)
Normanhurst School, Chingford

Graffiti

Scribbled, scratched or sprayed
Amazing work is made.
Like a way of expression,
As a beauty in words.
Spray paint or sticker
Graffiti is the way.
Art in public places and
The look on the Old Bills' faces.

Gangs come around the town
To get rid of that frown
The sizzling of pain
The wonderful sound
When you do it in the underground.

Our own little race in a public place.
The noise of boys when they spray in the shining sun
A tag of your name
Showing it without shame
But a fine you have to pay
But graffiti is the way.

Jacob Coy (12)
Normanhurst School, Chingford

Politics

This is my story to tell you the truth.
There are 5,000 leaders out there who are never scared
Everybody get up, this is the moment they are feared
Get up!
Show them you have got no fear
Get up!
Put your hands in the air.
There're some people out there who take advantage of blacks
Well I can tell you that black is back.
We are going to fight with all our might
And show them we have got no fear.

Nicholas Mesmin (11)
Normanhurst School, Chingford

Gangs

People in gangs . . . they think they are cool,
they think they are safe but they're not at all.
People in gangs they think they can't be fooled they are totally wrong,
they are easily fooled into doing wrong.

People in gangs why so much violence? Why so much badness?
Why so many ideas?
It's just all madness. People in gangs what can be done?
So many people wanting to join them.

People in gangs why can't you just stop?
I've lost my uncle because of a horrible lot.
People in gangs just what is the point?
I just don't know what they're thinking, these lot.

People in gangs why must it happen? Mugging, stealing and worst of all,
killing, why would you want to do that?
People in gangs when will it end? Threatening people, hurting your friends.

People in gangs when will it stop? My guess is never . . . hopefully I'm wrong.

Joseph Coley (11)
Normanhurst School, Chingford

Will He Ever Know?

He might never know
How much I love him so
He means the world to me
I see him every day, which lightens up my day

I know he knows I like him
I also know he works out at the gym
He takes the time to listen to me
I'm surprised he even does

I think of him as a brother
I know I won't have another
That's the way I like him
I love seeing him during the holidays
It lights up my world like anything else.

Yazmin Meikle (12)
Normanhurst School, Chingford

Poem

Please help, my child's gone missing!
Please help, I can't live without them.
They could be hurt, they could be dead
Until I find them I'll not go to bed.

I'm looking high, I'm looking low,
I just can't find then, which way do I go?
I've looked in the basement, I've looked in the loft,
Could they be next door, could they be down the road?

Oh please no, could it really have happened?
Could it be the worst, could they have been kidnapped?
This could be the end, they could be in a river,
They could be in a ditch, will I ever find them?

Wait, there could still be hope, we could find them,
They could still be alive
I'll call the police, surely they can help,
If they can't then I will yelp for more help.

Alexander Major (12)
Normanhurst School, Chingford

The English Weather

One day I was out in the sun,
My friend and I were having some fun,
When all of a sudden it started to rain,
We had to go inside again.

There I was inside my home,
My friend was there so I wasn't alone,
It's horrible outside as it was still raining,
But cosy inside so I wasn't complaining.

Thunder and lightning, a bang and a crash,
Watching through the windows the rain begins to lash,
Then the sun comes out, we go out to play,
We're so happy again, it's a beautiful day.

Declan Mead (12)
Normanhurst School, Chingford

A Soldier's Kit

Guns, our weapon
Gun to kill
Gun to protect
Gun to attack

Helmet, our head gear
Helmet to protect
Helmet to disguise
Helmet to shelter

Combats, our uniform
Combats worn with pride
Combats for camouflage
Combats our body armour

Boots, our footwear
Boots for marching north or south
Boots for stamping all about
Boots for walking in muddy trenches.

Oliver Swan (11)
Normanhurst School, Chingford

Love

Love isn't a big thing
Love's loads of little things
Like a kiss on the cheek at night
Or hugs in the cosy sunlight
When you're cold and he gives you his favourite jumper
Kisses in the rain
Hugging on the train
Everybody needs love
You only live once so take the chance now
Instead of never
YOLO = you only live once.

Holly Naicker (12)
Normanhurst School, Chingford

Egypt

A long hot day
As I lay
With the sun beating down
Turning my skin golden brown

Coloured fish of orange and pink
Make my eyes want to squint
Shark Bay is my favourite place
Even though the sharks love to chase

Sitting on the beach at night
Makes me want to sleep under the moonlight
Squealing away as I began to run
I pulled out a water gun

Different seashells lay on the beach
They all look a bit peach
The food gives you a bad stomach ache
It feels like an earthquake.

Sufyan Ali (12)
Normanhurst School, Chingford

School Poem

This poem is about every school,
And things that annoy people most of all,
Such as big mean teachers shouting in your face,
Don't you wish that they'd float into space?

Boring geography, with lame photography,
English reading sends me sleeping,
History lessons are horrible sessions,
And all the rest, they're not the best.

The reason why kids hate school,
Is because they're simply too cool!

Brandon Bennett (12)
Normanhurst School, Chingford

Justin Bieber

Justin Bieber is a boy who can sing.
Some people worship him just like a king.
Lots of girls think he's great
Whilst others give him lots of hate.

Born on 1st of March just a normal boy
To everyone's life he brings heaps of joy.
Justin Bieber is very kind
Others would say I'm being blind.

Fans will love him for ever and ever.
Some say that they will never.
For many girls he has taken their heart
A lot of boys want to tear him apart.

All Justin has to do is say, 'Hi'
Girls will burst into tears and start to cry
A lot of girls have the disease caused by Bieber
It has been diagnosed and is called Bieber fever.

Victoria George (12)
Normanhurst School, Chingford

My Victory

Lewis Hamilton is fast
I am faster
He's in my rear-view mirror
Coming closer.

Jenson button is in the lead
Not for long as I increase my speed.

Michael Schumacher is in his Mercedes
Cruising along not far from the finish
Before they know it, I've won.

Mohammed Usmaan Malik (11)
Normanhurst School, Chingford

Baby Sister

I first found out I am going to be a big sister,
Wouldn't mind if you was a little mister.

Can't wait to play with you,
And teach you how to use the loo,

Play with Barbies and do their hair,
I love you and will always care,

I never imagined this little sis,
And when you're born I'll give you a great big kiss,

You can wrap your tiny fingers around my thumb,
And I shall start calling you Sugarplum,

Soon we shall get a chance to meet,
And your little feet will smell so sweet,

Now your time is up,
And maybe we can do each other's make-up.

Lia Garcia (11)
Normanhurst School, Chingford

Boy Love

When you love a boy that is so close to your heart
You just feel a light, just take the love apart
Then you need a miracle to get it back again
You need total darkness to see him once again

He may not like me
He may love me
I may not be the one
But I can count on him like three, two, one
I need darkness to see you once again

We see each other every day
I will love you every day
If only you could talk to me every day

We see each other at parties
We see each other all day
I need a miracle to get it back again.

Hannah O'Shea (12)
Normanhurst School, Chingford

Mockingjay

Oh Katniss Everdeen from District Twelve,
The girl with a golden heart.
She tested the Capitol with nightlock berries,
A rebellion she did start.

The Capitol attempted to thwart her plans,
'Bring forth the Quarter Quell!'
As previous victors returned to fight
With the girl on fire as well

As Katniss struck her bow into
The arena outer wall
As for District Twelve, just minutes later
The bombs began to fall.

As Katniss became the Mockingjay
The Capitol did strive
To see her blood drip away
For Everdeen to die.

When war had ended she was given the bow and told
'Shoot President Snow in the head!'
She pulled the bow, the arrow flew,
And struck President Coin instead.

Jamie Powell (14)
Pencoed Comprehensive School, Pencoed

Rape

H – for hatred that I use deep down inside
A weapon struck into my parents' hearts
Who sold me to the clutches of the night
Who break and hid the virgins out of sight.
Destroying lives of those like me as they
Make us do thing, we scream that damn word
Rape!

U – for all the things that you will never see
And all the times and things you'd not believe
So nineteen million pounds it is the sum,
Of all those bodies paled, the deed is done.
And then my life became a huge train wreck
And I shudder when I hear that word
Rape!

Man – for well, if you can tell the male part of
My story which is just about to unfold.
They always think that they have got the class,
They also think that they have got the swag
They really think that they just have it all!
But they can shove their thoughts right up their a . . .
'Cause we still got the power and the soul.
And now I'm talking about the girls and boys,
And every single one who hears it
Rape!

The space between the two words represents,
The space between the two worlds; yours and mine,
And everyone just thinks of iPhone 5
While I am locked indoors to flirt with men
And be something I didn't want to be
The Lord can heal the world but seems not *me*
And chase away the world on my lips
Rape!

Traffic – for how long that I always have to wait
In line to live just like a prostitute
Before I knew it, it was my turn next
Those people with their evil little minds
They broke me, just as easily as ice
And afterwards they lashed and hit and hurt

For after that I screamed and screamed out
Rape!

King – for well what these 'pimps' think of themselves when
The rent us and get money in return.
They treat us like we belong to the floor
They look down right at us but then it's true
We're nothing to them but some little toys
Which they rent to others so they can play
With us until they break us, just as they
Did the Ten Commandments, and then we are
Again nothing to them but broken toys
That they themselves had broken just like they
Broke our virginity 'til we said
Rape!

Well they should know that kings will always have
An end of reign like human trafficking.
I've grown and tried to suppress memories
Of being locked in a room with desperate men
So let my story be a lesson to
All of you who think that strangers can help
Well that is all I wanted you to know
I hope you make sure that you heed my words.

Daisy Aje (12)
St George's RC High School, Worsley

Growing Up

When you are a baby,
You cannot walk,
You cry and you giggle,
And are learning to talk.

Then you are a toddler,
At year two or year three,
You're chatty and giddy,
And filled up with glee.

As you become older,
It's time now for some school,
Where you obey and play,
And start to learn rules.

After nursery and reception,
It's time for year one,
Where you start to get friends,
And have learning and fun.

After a few years of primary school,
You're now growing up,
You're going to high school,
And it's a *giant* close-up.

But there's nothing to scare you,
It's only children and more,
The excitement begins,
But the homework's a bore!

Once you're an adult,
You're getting a job,
It'll be what you want,
Of course not a slob!

Then there comes retirement,
You're getting old so relax!
It's time for some downtime,
You've worked to the max.

And that fatal day
Your life comes to an end,
You're a star in the sky,
You're a whirl in the wind . . .

Ellie Murphy (12)
St George's RC High School, Worsley

The Blissful Kiss

In the mist I feel the bliss upon my sun-kissed skin,
Sand blows by along with the pleasant breeze as the sun burns my chin,
I'm waiting for you patiently,
You're late for my expectancy,
The time is flying by along with the clouds in the sky,
Hoping for you to come before the night goes by,
Your words hurt me but I stay,
I want you, I need you every day
I hate you, we break up, you call me, I love you
What is this obsession I have for you?

You're eventually here after a long wait,
You sit next to me morbidly, you know you're late,
You're sorry, you say I love you,
My response is I love you too,
But really I'm thinking is this a lie?
I class you as mine, as you hold my hand.

The tide goes in, the sun goes far into the sky,
It's getting dark and that's when you awfully tell me it's all a lie,
I think of the bliss and ask for one more kiss,
Then run off sobbing into the mist,
Thinking of all the things I'm going to miss.

My anger swells up to my brain,
I don't react, but feel I'm about to explode,
I tell my mother, I'm in depression mode
And I burst into a million tears
A month of pain and sorrow, a month of sobbing in bed
A thousand emotions going through my head . . .

Lily Wilde (12)
St George's RC High School, Worsley

Seasons Of The Year

Seasons of the year, they bring us joy
Spring gives us a feeling of new beginnings
One's soul begins to sing at the fresh scents,
Life being born into a whole new world,
Plants and animals and the climate too,
They're all starting fresh in the month of spring

The month summer brings to us warmth and joy,
With families going on holidays
Beach resorts being packed with many people,
Children with large smiles on their faces,
They run around extremely frantically,
Whilst their scared parents try to hold them close,
Teenagers filling festivals happily,
They all scream loudly for their most loved band,
The older generation clean their gardens
They get ready for their new flowers to arrive.

Autumn has a feeling of death and cold,
As the lifeless leaves fall off the trees,
They're looking tired after a busy summer,
Their work is all done for the year,
Clothes get thicker as the warm weather fades,
And people's smiles soon turn into frowns,
Due to cold and windy weather returning.

And winter, the last season of the year
The season that finishes everybody's year off
The snow arrives and children play happily
They joyfully create large and round snowmen
They decorate it with a carrot for a nose
But never forgetting to keep it warm
They wrap him up with a woolly scarf
And later on, Christmas arrives
Many children write their Christmas list with hope
They anticipate on what they will receive.

And even though there is a feeling of ending
With the year soon drawing to a close
There is a feel of a new beginning
Natural things get ready for their work ahead
And people hope for good in the new year ahead!

Courtney Mather (12)
St George's RC High School, Worsley

YouTube – Good And Bad

YouTube is a site of beauty,
It lets me watch Call of Duty.
There's stuff like music, sports and more,
Including how to make a smore!

I like to watch a group called the Yogscast,
They make me laugh but it just ends too fast.
There's Lewis, Simon, Duncan, Sips and Sjin,
They have too many vids I can't begin.

Syndicate is another one,
His Minecraft Castle has just been done
Race to Prestige, Modern Warfare,
When facing hackers he takes care.

Sometimes there are ads which cannot be skipped:
I had an hour long ad – that's when I flipped!
People dislike because something was missed,
However in the description it's listed.

And on the other side are trolls,
Guys who spam ads and six-year-olds.
Trolls try to get channels removed
Fan bases have stopped them and proved.

Spammers may have good channels and content,
But their thousand comments show no relent.
There needs to be age limits on accounts,
Lots of high pitch vids – too many to count.

Oliver Lea (12)
St George's RC High School, Worsley

Homosexual

I'm homosexual, that's what I am,
But I'm no different still I am not man,
When I tell people I might be gay;
They turn their backs and always turn away;
It is not right and truly so unfair.

I'm sure I've learned and pained that you don't care,
The lies you said and told me you'd be there,
You promised me and swore it not to break.
Remembering the words that once you said.

We were best friends and laughed many a day,
But now I feel reject because I'm gay,
Now you are blind and me no longer see,
And I the truest friend since we were three.

Like rubbish you did throw me to the curb,
And left me on the street alone and scared,
For my life, now there's no one I can trust,
Why do you persecute me? I'm still me!

Come closer now because you need to hear,
It's not a person's choice to turn that way,
Our world is full of people who are gay,
And are proud to be and finally have their say.

Just go away and leave us gays alone,
Now hit the road and never come our way,
Our kind will never ever run away,
We stick together, we are very strong.

I know that gays will never hide from you;
Because we'll fight to stay on Earth today;
And even though we have performed no crime,
If you call us names, it won't make us cry.

I'll learn not to listen to nasty words,
Or care what names you think I might deserve;
We all live here with you on this planet,
So please think of sharing with us gays now.

Anna Marie Lindley (13)
St George's RC High School, Worsley

You Bullied Me

Well done you did your evil job
If that was to make me sob
In all those moments when I tried to hide
You gang and ambush me from every side
I'll haunt you every day
Until I have my say
In one way I'm glad because it made me stronger
The names just went on longer and longer
I remember the notes you used to pass
I remember the things you would spread around the class
The rumours you would spread were never true
I was not scared of the dark, just of you
One time for you I tried to hold the door
But then my lunch ended up on the floor
One day you went too far and o'er the edge
So then I pushed you right into the hedge
The teacher came and blamed it all on me
But when she finished I just ran with glee
The next day I came into school with a smile
But that didn't last a very long while
The next day you stole my shoes happily
I didn't care I'd had a victory
The next day you and your gang beat me up
And I decided that I was quite fed up
That's when I started to slit my wrists
I started to not care about your fists
My mum and dad started to get suspicious
That's when you started to get more vicious
After that I would start to fade away
One day in French I started to sway
Then I started to fall off my chair
And all those eyes started to stare
That night I ended my own life
With one cut from a single knife . . .

Emily Whiteley (12)
St George's RC High School, Worsley

Minecraft, The Beginning

The beginning

Minecraft is born as a world of brown and green.
Don't wait to venture into a world few have seen.
Collect some wood for tools,
I tell the truth when I say they aren't for fools.

Grab coal, gold and iron too,
Lapis, emeralds and diamonds for you.
Mine some stone to make a shelter,
Then put your treasure in the smelter.

Kill a pig, kill a cow, cook the meat till roasted
Quick before the night comes round
Before creepers blow us up – we're toasted!
Zombies, skeletons and spiders too
Run for your life or they'll come after you.

The sun rises,
No more zombies banging down my door,
A relief for the villagers, for they are so poor.
Trade with them until the emeralds are gone,
Since that is their only purpose, don't spend them for fun.

Build a city with blocks, one by one,
For that's the only way to get the job done.
If you feel the need to, then switch to creative,
Over 100 items for you to get imaginative with,
The blocks are unlimited so you can build for centuries.

With options of speed, swiftness and invisibility,
There is plenty to choose from to help with your ability.
But before I end this poem,
There is one thing you should know,
Minecraft is addictive,
It just won't let you go.

Joseph Shearer (12)
St George's RC High School, Worsley

My Poem

I woke up at 9.23, found the remote
So I could turn on ITV
There was a man called Jeremy
The only man for me
Same old story, my mother, I detest her
I need a lie detector.

I want a big mug of tea,
So does my stepdad who is called Lee
Bubble, bubble, bubble the water is boiling
Then I hear my mother calling.

'Darling, get out of your PJs
We have to go to Uncle Dave's'
I go upstairs and try to find something pretty to wear
Leggings or jeggings, oh sack it
I'm wearing my bright pink jacket.

'Hurry up hon', stop taking your time, it's not fun'
Mum is moaning again
Sometimes she is so very lame
Off I pop out of the door
In my pink jacket which I adore

The man on Jeremy Kyle was rather unpleasant
He looked like he was a peasant
I think he was called Keith
I remember he only had two teeth.

Angel Wilson (12)
St George's RC High School, Worsley

Acceptance

When the ghost of acceptance comes to play,
You pretend death is a myth and shy away,
Because you're too afraid to accept the fact that three zaps to this heart won't bring them back,
Because you know the dead are gone and the living none the wiser,
But all you do is wait, wait, wait,
But time can't heal the twisted fate.

Remember him in your year, called for being queer?
It wasn't there to guide their eyes to the writing written by the wise.
Remember how they never forgave you for your mistakes?
It couldn't be there to help them along the way.

Remember that quote; 'Only the strange and unusual can see me for I am the strange and unusual myself'.
It's strange to come around and unusual to be seen as Man has turned it into an object with no meaning,
So only they can see something they want, something they need, something they know could never be.

Now it's locked in its man-made 'home',
Waiting, waiting, waiting all alone,
In hope that one day there'll be a séance so its voice will be heard,
And its face known and no longer blurred.

Alyse Johnston (12)
St George's RC High School, Worsley

Women's Football

Football, the beautiful game for girls and boys,
But boys, like usual, think we should stick to toys.
They call us rubbish, they call us useless
If they carry on they'll end up toothless.

Boys expect free-kicks all the time,
Girls jump up and everything's fine.
Boys stress out when things don't go their way.
Girls do too but they don't like to say.

United boys get everything paid for them,
United girls don't, which causes mayhem.
Boys get trainers bought for when they go abroad.
Girls again don't, we sarcastically applaud.

We might be bothered about make-up and hair
But when it comes to football we don't care.
We go in for a tackle, we go in for a header,
When it comes to eating, we don't like cheddar.

But it is what it is,
And hopefully one day we could fight through this.
With the power of girls,
One day we will change the world.

Levi Rathburn (13)
St George's RC High School, Worsley

F.R.I.E.N.D.S

Are you my friend or are you not?
You told me once but I forgot
Best friends are wise, their spirit never dies
And moments, laughter, tears to soon follow

My friends and I have had our times
Some good, some bad, some happy, some sad
Our friendship is something we share
And I will always know you care

When I'm in pain I tell you all my fears
You always sit and join in with my tears
Our memories will never fade
I want to be forever friends

My friends think I'm a pain
But my best friend knows I'm insane
There's a time to hug and a time to cry
But there is no time I'll tell you a lie

If anyone hurts you tell me,
I'll make them cry and say bye-bye
We'll be best friends until we die.

Leah Calderwood (12)
St George's RC High School, Worsley

Friends Forever

Friends are like flowers,
They grow up together,
They pretend to be fairies
And dance around for hours.

They have their little arguments,
They usually don't speak,
But later on in a week or so,
They claim they're best friends forever.

They run around the playground,
And sing the whole day long,
They play some silly little games,
And try to write a song.

They go to each other's houses,
And play in each other's rooms,
They cry when it's time to tidy,
But they do it together very soon.

When it's time to wave goodbye
They sing, 'Best friends forever'.

Amy Louise Cannon (12)
St George's RC High School, Worsley

Little Big Soldier

I'm not afraid of those bullies,
Since I have my family and friends.
I'm not ashamed of not being able to defend myself on my own,
Having a helping hand is better than being alone.
Sometimes it's the other way round,
If you're lucky enough to see,
It may turn into World War III,
So we'll just have to battle each other to the ground.
Don't call me small, I know that already,
I'm pretty clumsy and not very steady.
I'm not that big physically,
But I'd say I'm quite strong mentally.
People mistake me for a china doll
Because I'm Chinese and kind of small.
I may look fragile and so very delicate,
But just watch out because I'm like a silent ninja that will put up any fight.

Just remember me,
I'm the little big soldier.

Kaitlin Kan (13)
St George's RC High School, Worsley

Seasons

The seasons, winter, autumn, summer, spring.
Winter, snow, frost and flakes.
Then all of a sudden spring breaks,
Refreshing scents of flowers, summer's all around.

After two months of sun,
Autumn waits to be found,
The leaves fall gently off the trees!
Summer is most popular by far!

I also love winter, oh the snow!
Winter, spring, summer, autumn, there you go!
Seasons come and go so fast,
But none were ever meant to last.

Lauren Bergin (13)
St George's RC High School, Worsley

Shopping

I love to shop it's really cool,
I'd love to choose my clothes for school,
I love to look around the shops,
And find a top with polka dots.
Teachers should let us wear our own clothes
But they forget we would feel more at home.

This won't affect our education,
We'll only seem like we're on a vacation
Of course we're not gonna rebel
But what we're gonna do? Expel?

They think we're gonna make fun of someone's shoes,
But they're not gonna be coming in dressing like the blues.
That's why at the dance we'll all dress up
And we'll be able to walk in our shoes, with luck.

Elouisa McManus (12)
St George's RC High School, Worsley

The Maze Of Emotions

Fragile as porcelain china that could shatter underneath your gaze,
Trapped in such a wild fantasy; a confused notion, the maze,
Breathlessly darting through each pathway only to find a closure,
Patiently she waits for some sort of exposure,

Each privet similar to the confined walls they caused her to build,
The essence inside of her, that spirit they'd killed,
Now, she remains as a corpse resembling form,
Her distraught structure twisted like a storm,

Hands tangled in her untamed mane,
Settling down on a nearby boulder a shock of pain
Jolted through her, originating from her hand,
Giving it a hasty glance, she notices blood dripping onto the land.

Chloë Povey (12)
St George's RC High School, Worsley

It's A Dog's Life

Little baby doggy, oh so sweet!
Naughty puppy, a few months old.
Not the shoes! One year old
Let's go for walkies! Two years old.

Oh how I love you doggy, three years old
I need to brush your fur, four years old
Oh you're getting older now! Five years old
A cute baby puppy from you! Six years old.

Oh you're not very well, seven and a few months
Oh where's my dog gone? Eight years old
She's dead!
Oh I'm very sad!

Ellie Smith (12)
St George's RC High School, Worsley

Litter

When I look around I see . . .
Litter everywhere
The amount I begin to despair!
People kicking cans
We need to make new plans

When I look around I see . . .
Muddy half-eaten chocolate bars
Piling way up to the stars;
It's a wonder it doesn't distract the cars.

When I look around I see . . .
Rotting old packets of crisps
Sometimes I even see apple pips
Littering our streets,
Our long, grey streets

Stop dropping litter!
I always jitter.

Helen Fraser (11)
Sacred Heart Catholic College, Crosby

I Believe . . .

I believed that the world had a better place of living,
But nowadays, people die every day
Some from hunger and some from pain
Why can't these people have a chance of living a different way?

Some countries but not all
Are endangered, this sounds to me as if they are animals
People treat themselves as species, but not just them, everything around them
Volcanoes explode, ditches pull and rivers break through even though there are lots of walls

I might be small but thinking of these incidents makes me a 1,000 times tall!

Some countries have no trees because most have been cut down
Why should this be true, you know what to do, save these innocent people and maybe harmless creatures
Kids don't need to be split up from their family, they don't have to be sent

Stop all the wars, *stop* all the floods
If all this doesn't stop who will be alive, who?
Don't let yourselves down
Do what you have to *do!*

Today the world is still in danger and to stop this mess we might even need a super ranger!

Even after this, you won't make at least three changes for the world
How can you possibly call yourself human?
Mother Nature, God
They can't do all the work around here
Hope is flying around the world today changing the world with the help of God, a true man.

Harrishina Raveenthirarajah (11)
Sacred Heart Catholic College, Crosby

Lions Of The World Unite

Butterflies are trying to flee
Fish are no longer in the sea
No more plums in the plum tree
Now it's down to you and me

There is no more lake
No slithering snake
A bird no longer awake
Look what we take

Monkeys have caught the flu
Cows are not going moo
Grass with no dew
You've got to help them get through

I'm the king of the forest
The mighty cat
I eat humans for breakfast
Now would you like a chat?

The jungle is nearly all gone
There is no sound and no song
What I hate about humans the most
Is how they're always wrong!

I have a family
Which you could save
Don't keep not caring about the rainforest
And please don't send us to our graves.

Robyn Martin (11)
Sacred Heart Catholic College, Crosby

Why Cut Down Our Forests?

What's the need, to cut down trees?
If it's bad then you're just sad,
If they go, then expect a foe,
All this is because of you.

The trees are moaning, widening and cracking,
The trees are falling all over the ground,
If you are standing then expect a landing,
All this is because of you.

The forest is called for peace at last,
So get out of the forest and sail with a mast,
The forest is driven to the back of the back,
Now it's your turn to leave a bit of slack,
If you don't then say goodbye,
All this is because of you.

Thank you, thank you!
You saved a forest
The forest is crying in happiness forever,
As we speak
The birds are squeaking,
The lion is roaring and the cheetah is snoring,
The forest says a sweet goodbye,
All this is because of you.

Daniel Waterman (12)
Sacred Heart Catholic College, Crosby

Is It Fair?

Why should some people be made to be hungry?
Who is so blind to say that is fair?
How can others be so selfish?
There's enough of this world to share.

I am just one amongst many and I may be small,
I will riot if I have to, to make these *people* heard,
But with my truth and heart I will stand up tall,
With the population of the world I will be prepared.

Somewhere a baby's dying and yet you sit there laid back,
They are humans like you or I,
War is not the answer, love is what you lack.
Injuries, death and illness and yet there you lie!

Reality is a jester toying with your mind,
Wealth, riches and power are tearing you apart
Love and kindness is how the human race should bind.
Maybe as a real globe we can make a new start.

I am hope and hope is in all of us,
My generation is full of proof to be rich
And the latest style and fashions,
But if one rises all will follow!

Campbell Wallace (11)
Sacred Heart Catholic College, Crosby

My Fur Family

My father's a suit, my mother's a dress,
My brother's a coat, my sister's a vest.
My family had they fought,
They may not be on a shelf ready to be bought.
If I was there maybe they would still be bears.

People say the bear is a fearsome beast,
But they just kill them to have a feast.
On their own they would not have won,
But they got help from a shotgun.

I am being hunted down,
So I do not have the time to frown.
My family funeral was short,
As I did not want to get caught.
Years later I will be dead,
But not by the cause of a pump of lead.

Why did god let them win?
My family did not live a life of sin.
Why did they take them instead of me?
I would die to bring back *my fur family.*

Daniel St John Eve (12)
Sacred Heart Catholic College, Crosby

Save Our Sea

The seas are going, the waves are slowing!
When they're gone, there'll be no song.
On a sandy plain, we'll be longing to hear it again!

The seas are bare, there was water there!
Why do we do nothing to keep it flowing?
How I wish they'd stay here, then we could all cheer!

The seas are going, the waves are slowing!
When they're gone, there'll be no song.
On a sandy plain, we'll be longing to hear it again!

How can you stand, looking grand?
Checking around, see the sand
Where did we go wrong?

The seas are going, the waves are slowing!
When they're gone, there'll be no song.
On a sandy plain, we'll be longing to hear it again!

The seas have gone, see everyone!
People help! Keep the kelp!
This is your future, *Save Our Sea*.

Peter Richards (12)
Sacred Heart Catholic College, Crosby

Fighting For World Peace

Feeling deep down under
With no thoughts in mind
Then I seem to wonder
Why some people are not kind

Think of Adolf Hitler
The one who started war
What cruel and harmful things to do
And ever so much more

Now think of John Lennon
He's the one who encouraged peace
He's the one to look up to
Because he wanted war to cease

The only thing I'd like
Is for all the wars to stop
And wars could go on strike
So peace and wars can swap

Let all thoughts be released,
Can you please help world peace?

Marcie Appleton (11)
Sacred Heart Catholic College, Crosby

Save Our Animals!

Help me save the animals,
The poor helpless things.
They deserve to be free,
Not made into bling!

The monkeys are happy swinging from trees,
They don't enjoy being locked up and you throwing away the keys!
The tigers are happy pouncing around,
The dolphins ecstatic swimming underground.

Why should this happen?

Gorillas are happy climbing about
But they are being trapped and we can't hear them shout!
Pandas enjoy fresh bamboo shoots,
Elephants enjoy nice juicy fruits!

Olivia Sansbury (12)
Sacred Heart Catholic College, Crosby

The Annoying Stepmum!

I ran upstairs with a thump and a thud,
I tried to explain but she misunderstood.
I scream and I shout but she still doesn't hear me,
I whine and I pine as she turns the key.

From banging on the door, my hands have blisters.
Why is she mean to me when she's nice to all my sisters?
Is it because me and my dad are always together,
I will love him for ever and ever.

She turns the key back and tells me to act normal,
She doesn't want Dad to know about all the kerfuffle.
I want my real mum back,
I am giving my stepmum the sack!

Ciara Moriarty (12)
Sacred Heart Catholic College, Crosby

No More War!

Please help me stop war, please help me stop war,
It kills lots of people and makes people poor.
Plenty of fighting means blood, guts and gore.
I don't agree with war – *no more war!*

It just begins with a silly disagreement,
How does something so little become something so big?
No one should celebrate, it's not an achievement
Don't sing and don't dance, don't jump and don't jig!

War is awful, how could you like it?
Instead we could be happy and peaceful.
I hate war – every little bit
Do I like war? No, it makes life less meaningful.

Ciara Robinson-Murray (12)
Sacred Heart Catholic College, Crosby

The Battlefield

Machine guns chatter
Hand grenades explode
Young men scatter
As the sound of guns reload
This is the battlefield
This is where the innocent and wicked die

Large craters appear in no-man's-land
Lifeless bodies lie limp in barbed wire
Blood stains upturned sand
For some the last they hear is the sound of a gun fired
This is the battlefield
This is where the innocent and wicked die

Family pray every night to see their loved ones again
Unfortunately for some they will never be able to do this
The last thing a relative wants to hear is their loved one's pain has been in vain
But the thought of having them home is bliss
This is the battlefield
This is where the innocent and wicked die.

James Hale (13)
The Crypt Grammar School, Gloucester

My Favourite Place To Be

Now guys listen, I don't want to sound sappy,
But this old place it can make us quite happy.
I know, I know, this is sounding lame,
But who'll be laughing when I have the fame?

When you guys are working in McDonald's
I'll be chilling with my eight models.
When you are asking if strangers would like chips,
I'll be sailing one of my many private cruise ships.

What are you doing when I'm in my manor?
Still in Year 8 correcting your grammar?
What are you doing when I'm out with Megan Fox?
Still making spaceships with LEGO blocks?

When you see me on telly hanging with the Queen,
There will be you wishing you were still a teen.
Should've retaken your GCSEs
But now you're asking, 'Will you give me a pay rise please?'

There's no need to pull our Brian's hair,
No need to take away Ollie's chair.
Don't copy Cian's work,
Go to the library, take out a book!

Don't barge Charlie in the corridor,
We all know you'll end up on the floor.
Forget calling Louis 'Four Eyes',
Get good grades, give you parents a surprise.

As you can probably tell,
I have done amazingly well.
This is because my favourite place to be. . .
Is the circus of course, silly!

Louis Claridge (12)
The Crypt Grammar School, Gloucester

Barmouth

Sand in my eyes,
Stuck to my thighs,
Lying in the sun,
It's so much fun.

Lapping over my feet,
The sea is such a treat,
Bodyboard in hand,
I feel like doing a dance.

Rides that make you dizzy,
Making you wish you hadn't just drunk that fizzy,
As you begin to hurl,
You fall over and curl.

Novelty shops all around,
The seagulls make a peculiar sound,
And when you go out for a meal,
I think you might begin to squeal.

This is Barmouth,
A city with an odd sort of smell,
With loads of natural resources,
Just sitting around.

So ask yourself this,
As you begin to yawn,
Is it all about the modern things?
And is the old stuff not modern enough?

I know a lot of people's answers to that question,
But the old things are nice once in a while,
That's the way this beautiful town is,
And that's the way (Uh-hu uh-hu) I like it!

Robin Trigg (13)
The Crypt Grammar School, Gloucester

Kingsholm Rugby Stadium

Watching Gloucester play
The crowd cheer
Whilst sipping a refreshing beer.
As Jonny May runs down the line.
The opposition are in disbelief as he looks so fine.

Burns steps up for the kick.
The ball flies so quick.
The ref blows his whistle; Sharples is near the corner and dives.
As all the opposition stand and sigh.

The ref blows, it's half-time.
The crowd cheer! Break time.
As they all dash to the bar.
Others think, *woah, that's way too far.*

As the game resumes
The opposition are doomed
The ball sails
The receiver fails.

On my God, what a hit!
The ref thinks that's it.
Reaches to his pocket
And out comes the yellow card.

The game is near the end
But Morgan comes in with the huge fend.
Pops it to Jonny May.
That's a Kingsholm day!

George Wheeler (12)
The Crypt Grammar School, Gloucester

The Sky

The shimmering sky,
Sun ablaze,
The birds fly high,
They're all a-daze

I look and admire,
At the blue morning sky,
It's a sight to inspire,
That's no lie.

Morning turns to afternoon,
The sun is high,
Women swoon,
At the wondrous sky.

Afternoon passes,
And soon comes evening,
The birds stop dancing,
The sun stops blazing.

The blue sky goes black,
Darker and darker,
In the harbour,
The sky goes black.

I suddenly realise,
I've been watching all day,
At the blue sky,
That's now gone grey.

Joe Robinson (12)
The Crypt Grammar School, Gloucester

Nevis Island Of Dreams

Rising out of the misty, blue sea the paradise island known as Nevis.
I step onto the silky white sand, as the sound of reggae fills the air.
I walk over to Sunshine's beach bar, he greets me and brings me a Ting.
I sit back and sip my refreshing Caribbean juice.
I instantly feel relaxed, as the warm breeze ruffles my hair.
The sun gently bronzes my pale white skin.
I rush to apply my sun screen, as I don't want to look like a lobster.
I am amused by the locals, as they try to start a game of volleyball.
It turns out to be the locals versus the tourists, but in the end it turns into football.
We decide to call it a day and head up to our house, looking out to the island's brother St Kitts.
The sun goes a deep red as it begins to set over the dark horizon.
The palm trees are silhouetted against the pink sky.
We go inside, as the deadly mosquitoes start to appear in the night sky.
The air conditioning has cooled the room and the sheets feel cool as
I slip into bed.
I watch a tiny lizard clinging to the wall trying to reach the window.
I fall asleep looking forward to tomorrow, awaiting the monkeys' screeches to wake me in the morning.
I cannot wait to go on a trek in the luscious, green jungle and explore the hidden parts of Nevis.
My mind is filled with the thoughts of the things I love to do here.
Snorkelling amongst the brightly coloured fish is one of my favourites, up there with fishing as well.
I drift off to sleep as the sound of my snores mixes with the sound of the tropical insects buzzing outside.

Cian O'Brien (12)
The Crypt Grammar School, Gloucester

St Ives Harbour

The glistening water,
The boats bobbing gently in the harbour,
The strong harbour wall still solid after hundreds of years of fighting the tide,
The soft golden sand,
Children playing and enjoying their young years,
The sun brightly shining,
The squawking seagulls swooping overhead, searching for food,
People sunbathing after hiring Rod's deckchairs,
People leaning against the walls,
The stone-formed arches along one side of the beach,
Fishermen tying and untying their boats
and climbing ladders with the day's catch,
The lifeboat poised and ready for any emergency,
The row of shops behind and around the harbour,
Gazing across to Porthminster beach,
A train going along in the wooded hillside,
The train appearing for a precious few moments before disappearing back into the tunnel,
Everyone knowing that in just a few hours
The sea will retreat and allow an afternoon stroll,
St Ives,
A true example of Mother Nature's beauty and
wondrous creations.

Harry Penny (12)
The Crypt Grammar School, Gloucester

My Favourite Place

Somewhere I can rest,
Somewhere I can play,
Somewhere I can stay all night and day.
Somewhere I can work,
Somewhere I can weep,
Somewhere I go, for a deep, deep, sleep.
Somewhere I can say everything is mine, my bedroom.

Charlie Pearce (12)
The Crypt Grammar School, Gloucester

England

The weather is bad
Why not catch some fish?
Inside your boots all you can hear is a squish
Come to England! You must be mad

The people have brains the size of a pea
Animals are no better, you'll soon see
On a sunny day you might get stung by a bee
Come to England! You must be mad

Their parks are easily the biggest I've seen
The scenery around is fairly green
Their laws are very mean
Come to England! You must be mad

A lion roars, a tiger growls
The animals in England struck dumb by a worm
All the population with their spades and trowels
Come to England! You must be mad

Now it comes to the final conclusion
My head cannot take the wild confusion
Would I come back?
In my brain I follow a track
It leads me to an answer . . . *Yes!*

George Burton (12)
The Crypt Grammar School, Gloucester

The Water Falls

The water calls,
From across the river,
The water falls,
Like an endless giver.

Splash! It crashes,
On the rocks,
Splash! It smashes,
By the docks.

So full of power,
The cascading water,
Falling from a rocky tower,
Like a giant sprinkler.

The water rages,
Off the cliff face,
For what seems like an age,
All the way down to the base.

Warmth travels through the breeze,
In the depts. Of night,
By the trees,
In the dimmest light.

Mohammed Shoieb Kholwadia (12)
The Crypt Grammar School, Gloucester

Any High Street

The place is *any* high street,
In the north, south, east or west.
The place is any high street,
Spot the difference, that's the test.

The place is any high street,
Where we don't have a voice,
We *have* to shop at Tesco's,
There isn't any choice.

The place is *any* high street,
A place to meet and greet,
But you'd better want a burger,
If you decide to eat.

The place is *any* high street,
Shop until you drop,
There will always be a HMV,
A Curry's and Top Shop.

The place is *every* high street,
They *all* look the same,
The place is *every* high street,
Which I think is a shame.

Harry Mutteen (12)
The Crypt Grammar School, Gloucester

World War One: No-Man's-Land

The guns rattled, peace has fled
War had begun and hundreds were dead
The atmosphere was murky, survivor wanted to go home
What were they doing there? This was no place like Rome

The ground was muddy and the sky was dim
Some had no experience so their chances looked slim
Hearts pounded, *thump, thump, thump*
As they ran through the trenches, ready to jump

The air was filled with shouting, as captains gave the orders
Soldiers were waiting to pounce over the borders
Running for their lives, through a thick blanket of smoke
The aim was to survive, this was no joke!

As emotions filled the sky, lives were stopped
Shells still going off as the injured flopped
Injured, impaired, survivors shattered
Cheers of victory echoed, as victory was what mattered

Finally, light broke through the dust and the fog
Lighting up the battlefield, there went the smog
The atmosphere changed, this was very sad
A day to remember, I survived and I am glad!

Tristan Beard (12)
The Crypt Grammar School, Gloucester

The Land Where Anything Is Possible

A world where anything is possible,
A land where whatever you fantasize can become true,
Where even mission impossible
Can seem like a zephyr for you.
You could go to America,
You could go to Iran,
What you need to remember
Is anything is conceivable in this land,
But you must be vigilant,
As a single erroneous move,
Can open up wormholes, this I do not suggest
As this can make your life
A blooming mess!
This wonderful land of clandestine,
This wonderful land of astonishment,
This place you cannot reach by cabriolet
This land is called the 'Internet!'

Louis Staley (12)
The Crypt Grammar School, Gloucester

Forests

I had friends,
We played in the trees,
Then they came,
First go the bees,
The saw has now come,
The trees fall up to their knees,
The man with the gun has now come,
There go the birds,
The man's laugh has now come,
So he can shoot them down,
Then here I come,
The lone monkey in brown,
Waiting for the worst to come.

Tom Willey (12)
The Crypt Grammar School, Gloucester

London

London is both
Historical and modern,
From the clock to the Olympic Park
From the loud audience to the loud chimes,
This is what London is all about.

Big Ben is there
Unable to climb,
Listen to the chime
And you'll have a surprise.

Busy plus loud equals London
In Stratford and in Leyton,
And everywhere in London,
Guaranteed you won't get a lengthy run on the streets of London.

Why is it so busy?
Cos it's a big, big city
Why is it so loud?
Cos everybody is speaking aloud.

Abdur-Rahman Dhalech (12)
The Crypt Grammar School, Gloucester

London

I walk every day under the heavy skies,
The grey lid that covers your people.
I walk through the filthy streets and step past,
Chicken bones, dog excrement, vomit, urine stains,
Cigarette ends, empty Stella cans, pizza boxes,
All discarded by you selfish people,
Who treat your crumbling streets with contempt.
London,
What have you left to offer?
You welcome the poor and treat them like animals;
You revel in your insular cockney aggression.

Aadam Goga (12)
The Crypt Grammar School, Gloucester

Jamaican Beach

The music never stops,
Whether it's day or night.
The bongos are the main instrument,
The music carries on with all its might.

The sun that beats down on the beach is unforgiving.
Many bathe in the sun,
With their sunhats and glasses they line the beach
in their millions.
Some are eating a ham bun.

The waves that wash up make a sound that's calming,
The pebbles make a rattling sound.
The sea is calm as it always has been.
The waves push the pebbles into a mound.

The windsurfing is immense.
And so are the waves that are surfed on in the sun.
Many competitions are held on those waves.
The competitions are lost and won.

Oliver Newman (12)
The Crypt Grammar School, Gloucester

The Moon

I look into the sky late at night
Just wondering about that heavenly light
It looks like a magical sphere
But as most of us know it has no atmosphere

The moon may be so far away
But it still affects our tides today
Several space travellers have already been there
Oh why can't I go? It's just not fair.

Scrape! And another lunar sample goes into the bag
Silence! There is no wind to blow the American flag
Broom! The astronaut drives off in his buggy
Screech! There's no need for brakes as it never gets foggy

Like many others I ask myself how it got there
I wonder if I will get an answer if I continue to stare
Now what would I buy after a huge lottery win?
It would be a first class ticket on a spaceship owned by Virgin!

Ryan Langstone (12)
The Crypt Grammar School, Gloucester

The World

I know a house, a cold, old house,
A cold, old house by the tree.
If I were a mouse in that cold, old house
What a cold, old mouse I'd be.

I know a street, a big, bad street,
A big, bad street by the school,
If I were a man in that big, bad street
What a big, bad man I'd fool.

I know a city, a slow, go city,
A slow, go city by the sea,
If I were a car in that slow, go city,
What a slow, go car I'd be.

I know a country, a grand, stand country,
A grand, stand country by alien zone,
If I were the capital of the grand, stand country,
What a grand, stand capital I'd be known . . .

Harry Fox (12)
The Crypt Grammar School, Gloucester

Life's Wonders

The person's life has many wonders,
You can have many wonders,
With friends and family,
In life there are many wonders.

You can live life how you like,
Have fun with scary wonders,
Or slow and funny wonders,
But all wonders are great.

Life will give you many wonders,
But you treat them differently,
You might laugh, cry, dance or whatever,
You have to remember you had that wonder,

Everyone should embrace their wonders,
Never reject a wonder!

Cameron Gallifent (12)
The Crypt Grammar School, Gloucester

Rugby

How can I sleep when I live what I dream?
I do what I love, I play for my team
Tiredness in my eyes
But feeling weak isn't the answer;
I need to pull out strength in me
And challenge myself and what lies within me.
It's a game where the limit is set,
The grass is pitched.
So I'm going out there and hitting the boundary,
My strength's having to be physical and mental
Shining bright, the sun's on my shoulders
The team's there, support's behind me
And I believe I can beat the person in front of me.
So pass the ball to me and let's play *rugby!*

Elliott Sharratt (13)
The Grays School, Grays

Family

My family inspire me to do what is best
They help me get through right and wrong
Sometimes I can be quite a pest
But they help me get along.

Family fun, fantastic fun, funny all the way
Miserable, moody, messy, oh what a day!

We can have our ups and have our downs
But we are still a family
There are smiles and there are also frowns
Living sometimes sadly, sometimes happily.

Family fun, fantastic fun, funny all the way
Miserable, moody, messy, oh what a day!

Life isn't always lived in the sun
We don't always feel happy and bright
We can still find a place for family fun
Turning the dark into light.

Family fun, fantastic fun, funny all the way
Miserable, moody, messy, oh what a day!

Time goes as quick as a blink,
Make the most of each day,
Listen to those around you,
And always have your say,

Family fun, fantastic fun, funny all the way
Miserable, moody, messy, oh what a day!

The truth might be hard to take
It's all about protecting each other
Remember to keep calm, for goodness sake!
At the end of the day, it's about loving one another . . .

Sophie Burcham (13)
The Grays School, Grays

Is Your War Really Right . . . ?

While you argue others fight,
For their country with all their might,
Everyone knows and everyone wants to help,
But is your war really right?

Making people fight for you,
From TV screen to blood-filled view,
The war they shouldn't be part of
Will hurt their families too

While you stay home under the sun
Soldiers are swapping their kids for guns,
So remember that when you start your war,
Swapping to strangers from their sons.

They fought and only some survived,
Going through those years deprived,
Missing all that was them and should have been them,
While you hide with your war obviously contrived.

Families mourn their loss,
Fields of stones holding a cross,
Next time you will think about if you're right,
As in your fields helpless bodies lie across.

While you argue others fight,
For their country with all their might,
Everyone knows and everyone wants to help,
But is your war really right?

Amy McDonald (13)
The Grays School, Grays

Freedom A Slave Wished For!

Freedom to think and freedom to know
Freedom to achieve and freedom to grow.
Freedom from struggle and freedom of ease
Freedom to enjoy and the ability to please.
Freedom from failure and freedom of success
Freedom from denial and freedom of access.
Freedom to live and freedom to die
Freedom to laugh and freedom to cry.
Freedom from hate and freedom of love
Freedom of below and freedom of above
Freedom from sickness and freedom of health
Freedom from poverty and uncontrollable wealth
Freedom from wrong and freedom being right
Freedom of the day and freedom of the night
Freedom to work and freedom to play
Freedom to believe and freedom to pray
Freedom to experience some day
I want to be free.

Terry Tabi (13)
The Grays School, Grays

In The Sky Late At Night

In the sky late at night are the stars
They shine so bright.

They dance and glimmer and sparkle away
I love to see them every day.

They glimmer and shine, they are divine
Oh how I wish they could be mine.

If there was one star I could keep
It would be the one that gives out heat.

Sirius would give out light
But that would make my room too bright.

So the stars must stay where they are
So everyone can admire them from afar.

Romy Daniels (13)
The New School at West Heath, Sevenoaks

The Life Of A Star

The young girl looks up at the sky
Once scared of the dark and all it held,
The hiding creatures of the night,
The nothingness of the darkness
Now comforted by the twinkling of the stars

The teenager looks up at the sky
Sitting on a blanket with her one true love,
As they share that first passionate kiss,
Dreams of being together for ever
With just the twinkling stars as their witness

The adult looks up at the sky
So alone after her first break up,
Crying tears that she thinks will never end,
Ignorant of the joy still to come
The beauty of the twinkling stars bringing her hope

The couple look up at the sky
Arm in arm in the garden of their first house,
They've been through so much,
Yet they've stuck together through it all,
The twinkling stars looking over them

The old lady looks up at the sky
Remembering what was, what had been
Friends that have long since departed
Now looking down on her from above
Each twinkling star someone she will never forget

The young girl looks up at the sky
Grandmother said the last time they ever spoke,
That she would be the brightest star in the sky,
Even after she had long gone
The brightest twinkling star

The twinkling stars look down on the world
They've seen so much, heard so much
The heartbreak and the sorrow, the joys and triumphs
The past and the present they've been through so much
Yet the twinkling stars know there is so much more to come.

Kerry Sildatke (16)
The New School at West Heath, Sevenoaks

A Soldier's Poem!

Fighting for queen and country, fighting for our nation
Fighting with courage, fighting with bravery and motivation
Our soldiers are spellbinding, our soldiers brave and pure
The only way of stopping our lads from dying, peace is the cure
Our soldiers at risk, at harm, our soldiers dying
War is the reason for this suffering, the reason to our crying
Thank you doesn't seem enough to say
When you're putting your lives at risk each day
Life so precious, life so special, so great
And yet our warriors risk it all, leaving life to fate
They do this for us, for their husbands, their wives
They do this for their mums, dads, for our country they risk their lives
Our saviours so special, I'm lost for words to say
So thank you to our young heroes for what you do each day
So young and yet so full of passion, bravery and motivation
So thank you for fighting for us, for our country, our nation
I'm so speechless, so lost but yet so proud
I'm going to sing your praise and I'm going to sing it loud
All of you are someone's child, someone's son,
Someone's daughter, someone's baby
So let our heroes home, just listen . . . just maybe
Respect is the work that I have left to say
Respect our courageous soldiers for what they do each day.

Sophie Dale (16)
The New School at West Heath, Sevenoaks

Stars

Stars, how they shine in the midnight sky, but I've always wondered . . . why do they shine so brightly?
Are they sad, are they happy? What is it that fuels them to light up the early morning sky?
I don' know, but whatever it is it fills me with both passion strong
and a sorrow deep.
A passion because they shine so strongly and brightly it makes you giddy.
Sorrow, because I know I will never shine as brightly as them . . .
Oh look, the sun.

Lee Barber (13)
The New School at West Heath, Sevenoaks

Star

Looking at the sky from the ground
The infinite blinking starry eyes
That everywhere surround,
The blackness of the night.

Each star its own story is living
It's light energy it's giving
To be the star that's noticed.

Each star looks down on mankind
And each man looks up at the stars
Then we dream because we can
We dream we are one of them.

They live, they die
Yet never eat nor feel
Each one cries out light
The light is the tears of stars.

Stars are nocturnal fires of the night
Hanging motionless on the canvas of black,
They shine hot, bright and white
They guide us through the darkness when we are blind.

Oliver Knight (14)
The New School at West Heath, Sevenoaks

Sky Bright

When I gaze up to the stars,
I sometimes wish I was on Mars.

The stars they twinkle and they glow,
And light the moon up far below.

I sometimes wish that I could fly,
And wave to them then say goodbye.

I know when morning comes,
They will fade away.

I will go to school,
And have a lovely day.

Harvey Ruske (12)
The New School at West Heath, Sevenoaks

The Keys

The stars they guide me to fate or fortune
I follow them whether they are right or wrong

The stars are keys they open and close doors
Some keys lead to great fortune or dark days
With every opening there is a closing
Some are happy, some are sad
Some lead to life, some lead to death

I watch the stars as they appear and disappear
There are always stars in the sky
I find my pathway in the stars every day and night

I fear the future and the past
I wish to read the stars
To know my day of death
I know it's soon so
I wish to find the final key.

Jacob Reynolds (13)
The New School at West Heath, Sevenoaks

Stars

Stars,
what are stars?
sometimes they are big,
sometimes they are small,
maybe they move with cars.

They shine bright,
they produce light,
they give you a fright,
stars elevate to new heights
maybe they just might, only at night,
who knows,
stars are wonderful!

Stéphane Noyelle (14)
The New School at West Heath, Sevenoaks

Written In The Stars

In the sky late at night,
The stars are shining nice and bright.

The moon comes out and lights the sky,
With a twinkle and a sparkle the stars come alive.

When the morning comes the stars go down,
The sun pops up and takes a bow.

The stars will sleep throughout the day,
Ready for the night when they come out to play.

Soon enough the night will come,
The stars will glisten for evermore.

Shelly Spikin (12)
The New School at West Heath, Sevenoaks

Sport Stars

Gold, silver and bronze are what we strive,
Lots of money just to arrive
A boxer's fee is won in the ring,
A sprinter starts with a spring,
Driving a kart and winning a rally,
Badminton horses riding in the valley,
England score, a cheer from the fans,
The national anthem playing by the big brass band,
When you score a point, one might knock at your door,
Everyone waiting for the final score.

Form 9Q (13)
The New School at West Heath, Sevenoaks

Stars

Stars are so bright in the sky,
Shines down and makes everything
In the night come alive,
Stars are so bright in the sky.

Sam Joyce (14)
The New School at West Heath, Sevenoaks

Stars

Stars shine, stars are bright in the sky, they are a speck of light
The more you will see the more you will wish for.
Stars of brightness lead the way to show the light in month of May
As the stars appear, you have no fear for they will shine all year.
You see a light gleaming bright in the sky up so high it's the star you wish upon
to make life live long.
The sight tonight gives you grief to show you what a star reflects
like under the reef.
May I say no more to this starry night
I shall leave them glowing in sky light.

Johana McEwan (14)
The New School at West Heath, Sevenoaks

What Are These Things In The Sky At Night?

What are these things in the sky at night?
What are they? They shine so bright
They fill the dark night skies up with light
My wish is to reach out and grab them, oh I just might
They're so close yet so far away
Will their twinkle last forever, or will it fade?
As I look out the window I see them glisten and shine
I look up to them and say, oh how I wish you were mine.

Claire Archer
The New School at West Heath, Sevenoaks

Colons

What is a colon?
My science teacher
Told me,
It digested my food:
But now I'm confused!

My history teacher
Told me,
Whilst studying World War II,
It is in fact a place in Germany!
Now I'm doubly confused!

My English teacher
Told me,
Whilst studying the grammatical laws,
It is in fact a dot on top of another dot,
Used to break sentences:
Not *wind!*
Now I'm triply confused!

I thought school was meant to educate me,
Not confuse me!
But that is what it appears to be doing.
Or is it just the English language,
At its best?
Maybe the French teacher
Will clear up my dilemma!

Toni Paxford (13)
Winterhill School, Rotherham

Galaxy

The galaxy's a mystery
Big bang created our history.
The stars above are nice to see
The Earth is part of the galaxy.
The twinkling stars are like a fantasy.
We're all just part of the galaxy.
When you look up at the stars above.
The shade of light is like love.
The swirling stars are like a track of cars.
When I look through my telescope I see Mars.
What a beautiful sight I can see.
I can't believe the Earth is part of the galaxy.

Giorgia Jade Cowie (13)
Ysgol Y Graig, Colwyn Bay

Young Writers Information

We hope you have enjoyed reading this book - and that you will continue to enjoy it in the coming years.

If you like reading and writing poetry drop us a line, or give us a call, and we'll send you a free information pack.

Alternatively if you would like to order further copies of this book or any of our other titles, then please give us a call or log onto our website at www.youngwriters.co.uk

Young Writers Information
Remus House
Coltsfoot Drive
Peterborough
PE2 9BF
(01733) 890066